ROUTLEDGE LIBRARY EDITIONS:
WORDSWORTH AND COLERIDGE

Volume 7

COLERIDGE AND THE ARMOURY OF THE HUMAN MIND

COLERIDGE AND THE ARMOURY OF THE HUMAN MIND
Essays on his Prose Writings

Edited by
PETER J. KITSON AND THOMAS N. CORNS

LONDON AND NEW YORK

First published in 1991 by Frank Cass & Co. Ltd.

This edition first published in 2016
by Routledge
4 Park Square, Milton Park, Abingdon, Oxon OX14 4RN
605 Third Avenue, New York, NY 10017

Routledge is an imprint of the Taylor & Francis Group, an informa business

Copyright © 1991 Taylor & Francis

All rights reserved. No part of this book may be reprinted or reproduced or utilised in any form or by any electronic, mechanical, or other means, now known or hereafter invented, including photocopying and recording, or in any information storage or retrieval system, without permission in writing from the publishers.

Trademark notice: Product or corporate names may be trademarks or registered trademarks, and are used only for identification and explanation without intent to infringe.

British Library Cataloguing in Publication Data
A catalogue record for this book is available from the British Library

ISBN: 978-1-138-67344-1 (Set)
ISBN: 978-1-315-56191-2 (Set) (ebk)
ISBN: 978-1-138-67011-2 (Volume 7) (hbk)
ISBN: 978-1-138-67012-9 (Volume 7) (pbk)
ISBN: 978-1-315-61778-7 (Volume 7) (ebk)

Publisher's Note
The publisher has gone to great lengths to ensure the quality of this reprint but points out that some imperfections in the original copies may be apparent.

Disclaimer
The publisher has made every effort to trace copyright holders and would welcome correspondence from those they have been unable to trace.

Coleridge and the Armoury of the Human Mind

Essays on his Prose Writings

Edited by
PETER J. KITSON
and
THOMAS N. CORNS
*University College of North Wales,
Bangor*

FRANK CASS

First published 1991 in Great Britain by
FRANK CASS & CO. LTD.
Gainsborough House, Gainsborough Road,
London E11 1RS, England

and in the United States of America by
FRANK CASS
c/o International Specialized Book Services, Inc.
5602 N.E. Hassalo Street, Portland, Oregon 97213

Copyright © 1991 Frank Cass & Co. Ltd.

British Library Cataloguing in Publication Data

Coleridge and the armoury of the human mind : essays on his prose writings.
1. English prose. History, 1800–1837. Coleridge, Samuel Taylor 1772–1931
I. Kitson, Peter II. Corns, Thomas N.
828.708

ISBN 0-7146-3426-3

This collection of essays first appeared in a Special Issue, 'Coleridge and the Armoury of the Human Mind: Essays on his Prose Writings', of *Prose Studies*, Vol. 13, No. 3, published by Frank Cass & Co. Ltd.

All rights reserved. No part of this publication may be reproduced in any form or by any means, electronic, mechanical, photocopying, recording or otherwise, without the prior permission of Frank Cass and Company Limited.

Printed in Great Britain by
Antony Rowe Ltd, Chippenham

Contents

Notes on Contributors		v
Abbreviations		vii
Introduction	*Peter J. Kitson* *Thomas N. Corns*	1
Coleridge as Critic	*John Beer*	4
Coleridge's Notebook Scribblings	*Kathleen Wheeler*	18
"The electric fluid of truth": The Ideology of the Commonwealthsman in Coleridge's *The Plot Discovered*	*Peter J. Kitson*	36
Coleridge, Kabbalah, and the Book of Daniel	*Tim Fulford*	63
"Murdering One's Double": De Quincey's *Confessions of an English Opium Eater* and S.T. Coleridge's *Biographia Literaria*	*Nigel Leask*	78
To "Make a Bull": Autobiography, Idealism and Writing in Coleridge's *Biographia Literaria*	*Steven Vine*	99
Coleridge against Romantic Autobiography: Charles Lamb's "Letter of Elia to Robert Southey"	*William Ruddick*	115

Notes on Contributors

John Beer is Professor of English Literature at Cambridge. His books include *Coleridge the Visionary* (1959), *Coleridge's Variety: Bicentenary Studies* (ed.) (1974), and *Coleridge's Poetic Intelligence* (1977); he has also edited Coleridge's *Poems* for Everyman's Library and his *Aids to Reflection* for the *Collected Coleridge* is forthcoming. In addition to books on Blake, Wordsworth and Forster he has also published extensively on a variety of authors.

Thomas N. Corns is a Senior Lecturer at the University of Wales, Bangor. He is the author of *The Development of Milton's Prose Style* (1982), *Computers and Literature: A Practical Guide* (with Brian H. Rudall) (1987), *Milton's Language* (1990), and numerous articles and papers, especially on Civil War prose.

Tim Fulford is a Research Fellow at Gonville and Caius College, Cambridge. He has been working on Coleridge for the last six years, and completed a Ph.D. thesis in 1988. His book *Coleridge's Figurative Language* was published in 1990.

Peter J. Kitson has lectured in English at Edge Hill College of Higher Education and the University of Exeter. He now teaches at the University of Wales, Bangor. He has published articles in *The Yearbook of English Studies* and *The Wordsworth Circle*, and is the editor of *Romantic Criticism 1800-25*. He is currently working on a study of religious radicalism from Milton to Coleridge.

Nigel Leask is an Assistant Lecturer at Cambridge University and Director of Studies in English at Queens' College. He is the author of *The Politics of Imagination in Coleridge's Critical Thought* (1988). His second book *Romanticism and the Interests of Empire* is forthcoming.

William Ruddick has taught at the Universities of Leicester, Dijon and Manchester. He has published on eighteenth-century topographical literature and painting, Scott, Byron, Hazlitt and Lamb. He is the editor of the *Charles Lamb Bulletin*.

Steven Vine is a Lecturer in English at the University College of Swansea, and is currently completing a book on Blake for Macmillan entitled *Spectral Visions: The Poetry of Blake*.

Kathleen M. Wheeler is a Lecturer at Cambridge University and a Fellow of Darwin College. She is the author of *Sources, Processes, and Methods in Coleridge's Biographia Literaria* (1980) and *The Creative Mind in Coleridge's Poetry* (1981), and the editor of *German Aesthetics and Literary Criticism: The Romantic Ironists and Goethe* (1984). She is currently completing a book, *Romanticism, Pragmatism, and Deconstruction*, and is engaged in preparing a *Blackwell's Guide to Twentieth-century Women Novelists*.

Abbreviations

AR	S.T. Coleridge, *Aids to Reflection* (London: Taylor & Hessey, 1825).
BL	S.T. Coleridge, *Biographia Literaria*, ed. James Engell and Walter Jackson Bate, *CC* 7 (1983), 2 vols.
BLS	S.T. Coleridge, *Biographia Literaria*, ed. J. Shawcross (Oxford: Clarendon P., 1907), 2 vols.
BPD	James Burgh, *The Political Disquisitions: or an Enquiry into Public Errors, Defects, and Abuses* (London: E. and C. Dilly, 1774–75), 3 vols.
CC	*The Collected Works of Samuel Taylor Coleridge*, Bollingen Series 75 (London and Princeton: Routledge & Kegan Paul and Princeton U.P., 1969–).
CL	*The Collected Letters of Samuel Taylor Coleridge*, ed. E.L. Griggs (Oxford: Clarendon P., 1956–71), 6 vols.
CM	S.T. Coleridge, *Marginalia*, ed. George Whalley, *CC* 12 (1980–), 2 vols.
CN	*The Notebooks of Samuel Taylor Coleridge*, ed. Kathleen Coburn [Vol. 4 with Merton Christensen] (Princeton: Princeton U.P., 1957–90), 4 vols.
C&S	S.T. Coleridge, *On the Constitution of the Church and State, According to the Idea of Each*, ed. J. Colmer, *CC* 10 (1976).
DQC	Thomas De Quincey, *The Confessions of an English Opium Eater*, ed. Alethea Hayter (Harmondsworth: Penguin, 1971).
DQR	Thomas De Quincey, *Recollections of the Lakes and the Lake Poets*, ed. David Wright (Harmondsworth: Penguin, 1970).
DQW	*The Collected Works of Thomas De Quincey*, ed. David Masson (Edinburgh: A.C. Black, 1889–90), 14 vols.
EOT	S.T. Coleridge, *Essays on His Times*, ed. David V. Erdman, *CC* 3 (1978), 3 vols.
Friend	S.T. Coleridge, *The Friend*, ed. Barbara E. Rooke, *CC* 4 (1969), 2 vols.
LL	S.T. Coleridge, *Lectures 1808–19: On Literature*, ed. R.A. Foakes, *CC* 5 (1987), 2 vols.
LPR	S.T. Coleridge, *Lectures 1795: On Politics and Religion*, ed. L. Patton and P. Mann, *CC* 1 (1971).

LS	S.T. Coleridge, *Lay Sermons*, ed. R.J. White, *CC* 6 (1972).
LW	*The Works of Charles and Mary Lamb*, ed. E.V. Lucas (London: Methuen, 1903–05), 7 vols.
MPW	*The Complete Prose Works of John Milton*, ed. D.M. Wolfe (New Haven: Yale U.P., 1953–83), 8 vols.
NB	S.T. Coleridge, Unpublished Manuscript Notebooks.
NQ	*Notes and Queries*.
PL	*The Philosophical Lectures of Samuel Taylor Coleridge*, ed. Kathleen Coburn (London and New York: Pilot Press, 1949).
PW	*The Poetical Works of Samuel Taylor Coleridge*, ed. E.H. Coleridge (Oxford: Clarendon P., 1912), 2 vols.
TT	*Table Talk and Omniana*, ed. T. Ashe (London: George Bell, 1888).
TWC	*The Wordsworth Circle.*
Watchman	S.T. Coleridge, *The Watchman*, ed. L. Patton, *CC* 2 (1970).
WPrW	*The Prose Works of William Wordsworth*, ed. W.J.B. Owen and J.W. Smyser (Oxford: Clarendon P., 1974), 3 vols.
WPW	*The Poetical Works of William Wordsworth*, ed. E. de Selincourt and Helen Darbishire (Oxford: Clarendon P., 1940–49), 5 vols.

Introduction

> For language is the armoury of the human mind; and at once
> contains the trophies of its past, and the weapons of its future
> conquests. (*BL* 2: 30–1)

With the publication, this year, of Coleridge's *Table Talk*, the grand project of *The Collected Works* approaches completion. The *Collected Works* is scheduled to run to some 22 volumes and these, combined with the five large volumes of the *Notebooks* (volume 4, covering the years from 1819 to 1826, has just appeared), demonstrate the vastness and depth of Coleridge's interests and understanding, and the importance of his achievement.[1] If E.K. Chambers' judgement of "the Sage of Highgate" made in 1939 – "So Coleridge passed, leaving a handful of golden poems, an emptiness in the heart of a few friends, and a will-o'-the-wisp light for bemused thinkers" – was ever taken seriously, it has been well and truly repudiated by the availability of Coleridge's work in these scholarly and meticulously annotated editions.[2] Even a cursory glance at the lists of academic publishers will show that Coleridge's life and work continue to fascinate scholars from different generations and diverse methodological backgrounds.

The essays collected in this volume bear witness to the continued interest that Coleridge holds for scholars of Romanticism and they demonstrate the extraordinary variety and fecundity of Coleridge's work. Among the essays are studies of Coleridge's literary criticism, his early political and prophetic writings, his "metadiscursive" methods, and his experiments in Romantic autobiography. From reading this special issue of *Prose Studies* we can gain some impression of Coleridge's "myriad-mindedness" (a term he applied to Shakespeare) and also of the central importance he had to his contemporaries as an interpreter of the signs of the times. William Hazlitt, an originator of the view of Coleridge as a lost leader, never doubted his erstwhile idol's prodigious intelligence. In his *Lectures on the English Poets* (1818), he wrote of Coleridge as "the only person I ever knew who answered to the idea of a man of genius," and John Stuart Mill much later described Coleridge with Bentham as "the two great seminal minds of England in their age."[3] Leaving aside the question of Coleridge as a great poet who produced some of the most memorable and resonant poetry in English, his political, philosophical and religious writings were highly influential during his age and beyond. Perhaps it was the form in which Coleridge composed his prose writings which led to the earlier misreading of the nature of his genius. As John Beer points out, in the opening essay of this collection, beyond the major published work such as *The Watchman, The Friend, Biographia Literaria*, the *Lay Sermons, Aids* to *Reflection*, and *On the Constitution of the Church and State*, many of Coleridge's most important and interesting critical statements were made in the form of lectures and essays published after his death, notebooks, marginal comments, recorded conversations and, especially, letters. It is in many of these irregular writings that Coleridge is at his most characteristic and suggestive. The essays in this volume make good use of such writing: Kathleen Wheeler traces the original notebook entries behind some of Coleridge's most famous published statements; Tim Fulford draws on unpublished notebooks in unravelling Coleridge's complex relationship between prophecy and the Kabbalah; and Peter Kitson alludes to a Sermon Coleridge gave in 1799 which still, in its entirety, remains unpublished. All the contributors make use of the letters of Coleridge or his contemporaries. Indeed many of Coleridge's letters themselves constitute mature critical or philosophical positions. Although, like Byron, Coleridge always seems to be aware of the standpoint of the recipient of his letters when formulating his own position, many of them would stand on their own merits as substantial essays; in particular, one thinks of the autobiographical letters to Poole, the philosophical letters to Thomas Wedgewood, and the political and literary letters to Thelwall and Sotheby. John Beer elegantly uses the letters to Southey, Thelwall, Sotheby, and others to demonstrate the development of Coleridge's critical thought towards his ideal of uniting the head with the heart.

The "notebook scribblings" of Coleridge are deployed by Kathleen Wheeler to show how he adopts the classical rhetorical strategy of "hypotyposis," which is akin to our modern notion of metadiscourse, in the difference between the "occasional jottings" (notebooks, marginalia, and sometimes, but rarely, letters) and their manifestation as published writing in which Coleridge encourages the reader to participate emotionally and reflectively in the text. Kathleen Wheeler provides a rich and fascinating examination of the metamorphosis of some of Coleridge's most characteristic images, such as the serpent-like motion of the imagination, the lustre of the calm lake, concealing depth, and the polarity of thought. Both Peter Kitson's article and that of Tim Fulford discuss some of the Bristol lectures of the young Coleridge, and show his interest in the prophetic mode. Kitson argues for the subtlety and richness of the strategies Coleridge develops in his political pamphlet *The Plot Discovered*, which harks back to the golden age of the polemic of the Puritan Revolution, and Tim Fulford grounds his discussion of Coleridge's interest in the prophecy of Daniel on Coleridge's response to Paine's demystification of prophecy. Fulford shows how Coleridge abandoned the conjectural millenarianism of his youth, preferring instead the notion of symbolic narrative as a hermeneutic model. His understanding of the prophecies was deepened by his continuing awareness of the writings of the Kabbalah.

The very modern preoccupation with the nature of the self is shown to be an issue in Coleridge's writings by the contributions of Nigel

Leask and Steven Vine. Concentrating on that great and enigmatic Romantic autobiography, *Biographia Literaria*, both writers show the text's concern with the identity of its subject. Nigel Leask vividly depicts De Quincey's attempt at autobiography as both an interpretation and a challenge to Coleridge's own "exculpation" of his literary life and opinions in the *Biographia*. Both autobiographies are written against the background of drug addiction and both grapple with the problems of the literary representation of the self and its relationship to the personal identity of the writing subject. Leask's discussion of Coleridge's account of making a "bull" in chapter 4 of the *Biographia* leads into Steven Vine's reading of the same figure. Vine shows Coleridge's attempts to gather his own scattered literary products into a metaphysical subjectivity which allows the unity of the self, as a personal and a written subject. William Ruddick also deals with Romantic autobiography, viewing Charles Lamb's response to Southey's criticism of *Elia* in the context of Coleridge's ideas on biography from *The Friend*. Ruddick amply illustrates Coleridge's contribution to the current debate about what constitutes a biography, and describes Romantic autobiography in the larger context.

In a famous and oft-quoted phrase, Coleridge, referring to the work of Kant, told how "until I understand a writer's Ignorance, I presume myself ignorant of his understanding" (*CL* 5: 14). The essays in this issue show that most of us have a long way to go before we are in a position to master even the basics of Coleridge's substantial and expansive thought. What is clear, however, is that there will always remain many scholars, intrigued, fascinated, and even, like the Wedding Guest, spellbound by the complexity and insight of Coleridge's work.

PETER J. KITSON
THOMAS N. CORNS

NOTES

1. S.T. Coleridge, *Table Talk*, ed. Carl Woodring, *CC* 14 (1990), 2 vols.; *The Notebooks of Samuel Taylor Coleridge*, vol. 4: *1819–1826*, ed. Kathleen Coburn and Merton Christensen (Princeton: Princeton, U.P., 1990), 2 parts. See Abbreviations.
2. E.K. Chambers, *Samuel Taylor Coleridge: A Biographical Study* (Oxford: Clarendon P., 1939), 331.
3. *Mill on Bentham and Coleridge*, intro. F.R. Leavis (London: Chatto & Windus, 1967), 40.

Coleridge as Critic

The judgment that Coleridge was the most important English critic of his age is, in the end, hard to resist. But where exactly did his greatness lie? Normally one expects from a critic a series of books or treatises through which a thread of consistency can be discerned or at least readily identifiable major statements in which (as with his great German contemporary A.W. Schlegel) positions are advanced and subsequently developed or ramified.

With Coleridge it is different. The one major critical book published in his lifetime, *Biographia Literaria*, was not presented as such and is digressive and unpredictable in its arrangement. Beyond that we have sets of lectures and essays published after his death, together with critical judgments scattered in short essays, notebooks, marginal comments, recorded conversations and letters. Leading ideas and central passages can be located, seminal thoughts traced; yet it remains the case that a reader coming to Coleridge for the first time may be bewildered. And when some of the passages of unacknowledged borrowing are discovered another suspicion may be aroused: did he after all take all his main positions from German criticism?

Faced with this situation it may be helpful to approach *Biographia Literaria* more obliquely. Instead of reading it in the way that it is presented, as a literary autobiography, we need to develop our own method of genetic criticism. Tracing the progress of Coleridge's critical statements through his early years makes it possible to detect certain contradictory strains and so to see more clearly the nature of that brilliant but strangely riven document.

The characteristics of Coleridge's mind early disclosed themselves as ill-attuned to those of the immediately preceding period, with its taste for large schematisations. By comparison with the underlying single-mindedness encouraged by such a search, his psyche was shifting and versatile. The epithet which he applied to Shakespeare, "myriad-minded,"[1] was evidently one that he would have liked to apply to himself as well. As a result he early learned the need to develop different kinds of discourse, in correspondence with strains in his own psyche.

He had his predecessors, of course. One can already trace something of the kind in Johnson's habit of blending a discourse of nature and a discourse of morality. Later, Matthew Arnold was to adopt a similar mode as he made the case for a blending of Hellenistic and Hebraistic values. There is no great problem here, however, since the nature of the discourses is easy to discern. With Coleridge by contrast, the tendency to move between such discourses means that those who are looking for some uniting singleness may soon find themselves bewildered. For it is not simply a matter of two or three clearly defined and clearly understood discourses that can be traced throughout a writing that has its own homogeneity. In Coleridge the interrunning of discourses formed a way of writing that ran so deep as not always to be fully under his own control. His main aim was to bring everything he had to say into a single harmonised pattern, and while he was remarkably good at this in local instances an element of legerdemain or of uneasiness can sometimes be detected, as if he were aware that fissures were opening out in what he was trying to bring together.

Few writers begin their careers with the intention of making literary criticism their profession, and Coleridge was no exception. The indications, in fact, are that his original plans were quite different. At first he was intended for the Church, and any plans to write would have been comprised within that vocation, following an honourable tradition that had included figures as diverse as John Donne, George Herbert, Jonathan Swift and Edward Young. In the 1790s, under the stimulus of the French revolution, his ambitions changed direction. At that point the most pressing need seemed to him to be to find a progressive but non-violent alternative to what had happened in France. For a time he followed the lead of Joseph Priestley, who had succeeded in being at one and the same time religious dissenter, political radical and innovative scientist: an early hope, to be traced particularly in his early poem "Religious Musings," was that he would be a prophet for the age, following the tradition of Milton while taking into account all the developments in knowledge since the seventeenth century.

If that stance could authorise many activities in the 1790s, literary criticism was not prominent among them. His critical position, so far as he had one, can be found in a letter he wrote in 1796 to Thelwall, the political activist, where it emerges directly from an attempt to justify the kind of poetry he was currently writing:

> I feel strongly, and I think strongly; but I seldom feel without thinking, or think without feeling. Hence tho' my poetry has in general a *hue* of tenderness, or Passion over it, yet it seldom exhibits unmixed & simple tenderness or Passion. My philosophical opinions are blended with, or deduced from, my feelings: & this, I think, peculiarizes my style of Writing. And like every thing else, it is sometimes a beauty, and sometimes a fault. But do not let us introduce an act of Uniformity against Poets – I have room enough in *my* brain to admire, aye & almost equally, the *head* and fancy of Akenside, and the *heart* and fancy of Bowles, the solemn Lordliness of Milton, & the divine Chit chat of Cowper: and whatever a man's excellence is, that will be likewise his fault. (*CL* 1: 279)

When Coleridge's career began to complicate itself in the following year two factors were prominently involved. One was his growing disillusionment concerning the possibilities of political action as he contemplated the hardening of political attitudes in Britain, along with the very marginal impact made by his periodical *The Watchman* even in the limited progressive circles where he could best hope for a sympathetic response. The demand had proved small and vacillating. And at the same time he was turning increasingly to the one man who seemed to him to be indisputably possessed of major poetic powers: William Wordsworth.

If Coleridge had not met Wordsworth it is hard to guess what might have happened. He would no doubt have continued to devote himself for longer than he did to the cause of radical thinking, replacing political activity by intellectual, and trying to relate the latest developments in science to what had come to be known of ancient tradition through the mythological and religious researches of his contemporaries and predecessors.[2] In his attempt to educe a living tradition which could form the core of a revitalised Christianity he might well have continued to look to the Unitarians of the time, along with various figures who were pursuing scientific investigations. A good deal of documentation was now available concerning ancient philosophies and other religions, while the new experimentation that had recently begun in Bristol with Thomas Beddoes and Humphry Davy offered further scope for such free enquiry.

There are signs, indeed, that Coleridge continued to think in this manner for a time. But the most important factor in giving direction to his thought, the relationship with Wordsworth, was moving it in a different direction. Wordsworth, who had suffered a deeper political disillusionment than Coleridge, was turning his thoughts less to science than to the immediate impact of nature, and particularly the influences on humanity provided by living close to it. Coleridge, in turn, was fired by this way of making concrete his preceding intellectual concerns. For a time, indeed, both men were evidently exchanging ideas so rapidly and intensely that some could be said to emerge from the relationship rather than from either participant in it.

One major effect on Coleridge's writing had soon become evident: his favourite habit of thinking about nature in terms of vivid mental images derived from his reading gave way to a concentration rather on Nature's sensuous detail – a manner of writing for which he had already shown a gift in his early poem "The Eolian Harp." And this meant he was considering the nature of life in a more direct way, looking at nature and asking himself just what in it, viewed directly rather than through the eye of the scientific experimenter, could be thought to constitute our sense of the nature of life at the most general level.

This feature, which comes out in Coleridge's meditative poetry, began to enter his criticism as well, prompting him to look at the literary works of others for their signs of organic life. He further explained what was in his mind by criticising the great available model for thinking about nature generally that had been offered by Newton. In this case, he believed, the attitude of the observer was conceived wrongly:

> *Mind* in his system is always passive – a lazy Looker-on on an external World. If the mind be not *passive*, if it be indeed made in God's Image, & that too in the sublimest sense – the Image of the *Creator* – there is ground for suspicion, that any system built on the passiveness of the mind must be false, as a system. (*CL* 2: 709)

Alongside this a favourite sentence (which he may even have been using when he was in Germany in 1798–99), "Every Thing has a Life of it's own, and ... we are all one Life,"[3] provided a telling brief statement of his own particular philosophy.

These two formulations help us to catch something of an idea that had been impressing itself more and more on Coleridge's thinking in the previous years: that there appeared to be two levels to human consciousness: one the attentive waking concentration in which we focus upon outward objects and try to understand them through observation, the other the passive subconscious processes by which we relate the life-processes in ourselves to those of other people – and indeed of all living beings. The one level of consciousness is realised most extremely in cold analysis of the external world, the other in a warm empathy with other organisms. Somewhere between there occurs that mediating state of consciousness in which, to quote Wordsworth's words in "Tintern Abbey," "We see into the life of things."

To learn to think in this complex fashion did not simply affect Coleridge's view of nature; inevitably it affected his view of literary creation, and so, by a natural progression, his literary criticism. Some of his subsequent thinking on these lines evidently went into the Preface to *Lyrical Ballads* in the edition of 1800, where a notebook phrase of his, "recalling of passion in tranquillity," is echoed in the famous "emotion recollected in tranquillity."[4] There are signs that he was thinking more and more in terms of psychological investigation and its relationship to poetry, still clinging to his affirmation that the age needed a joint working of head and heart – of intellect and the emotions. One of his aims in writing *Christabel*, he said later, was to try a new metric principle, "counting in each line the accents, not the syllables." "Nevertheless," he declared, "this occasional variation...is not introduced wantonly, or for the mere ends of convenience, but in correspondence with some transition in the nature of the imagery or passion."[5]

It was in 1802, when he had left behind journalistic work and scientific speculation in order to live in the Lake District and devote himself to the development of his own ideas, that his thinking in this manner became truly complex and pervasive. As Wordsworth approached his marriage to Mary Hutchinson he wrote, in an extraordinary burst of productivity, "The Rainbow," the Immortality Ode and many other poems celebrating his life with Dorothy in Grasmere. Coleridge shared something of that feeling but it was darkened both by the negative recognition that such a way forward was not available to him and by a suspicion that the beneficent working of nature was not so straightforward a matter as Wordsworth was suggesting. The writing of "Dejection: An Ode" was his response. Yet although he might in that poem lament the fact that his "shaping spirit of imagination" appeared to have deserted him – at least for the time being – the very writing of the poem showed other elements in his poetic powers to be still strongly active. This was reflected in his comments on poetry during the summer. In a letter to Sotheby of 13 July Coleridge wrote about the need for every phrase, every metaphor, every personification to have its justification in "some *passion* either of the Poet's mind, or of the Characters described by the Poet." "But *metre itself*," he continued, "implies a *passion*, i.e. a state of excitement, both in the Poet's mind, & is expected in that of the Reader" (*CL* 2: 812). At the end of the same month he quoted to Southey Milton's praise of poetry that was "simple, sensuous and passionate" (29 July 1802; *CL* 2: 830).

Elsewhere in the letter to Sotheby he criticised the continental poetry of the time, proceeding into one of the finest pieces of general criticism he ever wrote. The full implications of the "one Life" as a criterion for poetic making emerged to the full as he explained what he thought made a great poet, locating it in an ability to live in the lives of others:

> It is easy to cloathe Imaginary Beings with our own Thoughts & Feelings; but to send ourselves out of ourselves, to *think* ourselves in to the Thoughts and Feelings of Beings in circumstances wholly & strangely different from our own/ hoc labor, hoc opus/ and who has atchieved it? Perhaps only Shakespere. Metaphisics is a word, that you, my dear Sir! are no great Friend to/ but yet you will agree, that a great Poet must be, implicitè if not explicitè, a profound Metaphysician. He may not have it in logical coherence, in his Brain & Tongue; but he must have it by *Tact*/ for all sounds, & forms of human nature he must have the *ear* of a wild Arab listening in the silent Desart, the eye of a North American Indian tracing the footsteps of an Enemy upon the Leaves that strew the Forest – ; the *Touch* of a Blind Man feeling the face of a darling Child – / and do not think me a Bigot, if I say, that I have read no French or German Writer, who appears to me to have had a *heart* sufficiently pure & simple to be capable of this or any thing like it. (13 July 1802; *CL* 2: 810)

Those sentences offered one programme for a kind of writing that the age was looking for, a programme which was to some degree to be fulfilled by his successors. At the same time they run counter to some of the most dearly-held positions of a later criticism. A New Critic would have been deeply disturbed by the presuppositions they contain, for they suggest an ability to get inside other minds which was later to be regarded as impossible, and in any case inappropriate to the purposes of literary judgment. Coleridge, concerned to escape the tyranny of a rule-bound poetry and to bring about the unification of head and heart that was persistently his ideal had no such reservations. On the contrary, the kind of poetry he was proposing had for him the further virtue of guarding against self-enclosure and self-regard. He returned to the theme in another letter to Sotheby, written in September of the same year, in which he expressed his disappointment at the contents of the latest volume published by his former poetic hero, William Lisle Bowles:

> There reigns thro' all the blank verse poems such a perpetual trick of *moralizing* every thing – which is very well, occasionally – but never to see or describe any interesting appearance in nature, without connecting it by dim analogies with the moral world, proves faintness of Impression. Nature has her proper interest; & he will know what it is, who believes & feels, that every Thing has a Life of it's own, & that we are all *one Life*. A Poet's *Heart & Intellect* should be *combined, intimately* combined & *unified*, with the great appearances in Nature – & not merely held in solution & loose mixture with them, in the shape of formal Similies. (10 September, 1802; *CL* 2: 864)

This did not of course signal a retreat from moral considerations as such. On the contrary, in this year Coleridge was facing the fact that his own moral principles would not permit him to abandon his marriage. And in spite of his high valuation of poetry in which we "send ourselves out of ourselves," he could not allow his desire to enter into the lives of others to proceed so far as to indulge a free flow of thought without any kind of self-restraint. In view of its naturalism one might have thought that he would have been drawn at this time to Greek art and poetry, but he was not. When he returned to these questions months later, in another letter to Sotheby, it was another literature that he invoked as exemplary of the sublime in nature:

> It has struck [me] with great force lately, that the Psalms afford a most compleat answer to those, who state the Jehovah of the Jews, as a personal & national God – & the Jews, as differing from the Greeks, only in calling the minor Gods, Cherubim & Seraphim – & confining the word God to their Jupiter. It must occur to every Reader that the Greeks in their religious poems address always the Numina Loci, the Genii, the Dryads, the Naiads, &c &c – All natural Objects were *dead* – mere hollow Statues – but there was a Godkin or Goddessling *included* in each – In the Hebrew Poetry you find nothing of this poor Stuff – as poor in genuine Imagination, as it is mean in Intellect – / At best, it is but Fancy, or the aggregating Faculty of the mind – not *Imagination*, or the *modifying*, and *co-adunating* Faculty. This the Hebrew Poets appear to me to have possessed beyond all others – & next to them the English. In the Hebrew Poets each

Thing has a Life of it's own, & yet they are all one Life. In God they move & live, & *have* their Being – not *had*, as the cold System of Newtonian Theology represents/ but *have*. (*CL* 2: 865–6)

In this passage we can sense one of the double strains of discourse discussed earlier. They had been evident from Coleridge's early years, emerging, starkly exposed, in his 1795 poem "The Eolian Harp." But at this point he was trying to interweave the strands more subtly – in a manner more reminiscent of Arnold's running together of Hebraism and Hellenism. In his case no concessions were to be made to Hellenism, but the attempt to run together an appeal to righteousness and to the imaginative was not dissimilar.

From one point of view the two clearly pull apart, since the linking of imaginative experience with sensuous attraction might seem Hellenic in quality. What holds the two elements together in Coleridge's mind, on the other hand, is his belief in a continuity between the inward being of the human psyche, the inward being of nature and the inward being of God. And this, of course, he expected to find reflected in the work of the creative imagination, which he believed to represent, in however limited and imperfect a fashion, the creative power of the divine. While the introduction of Hebrew poetry as an ideal might seem to be constraining the range of Coleridge's thought within the domain of righteousness, this other, secret bonding between the levels of his thought guarded him from having to draw that conclusion too readily.

During these years, when there was a struggle between his creative imagination and his moral imagination, the creative imagination was always likely to gain a subterranean victory. In terms of his successive statements on critical issues this meant that once a statement had been made which blended imaginative and moral discourses it was the creative imagination that was likely to continue working and to produce the germ of the next statement. In the passage I have just cited from the letter of September 1802, for example, there is an important distinction half-buried in the run of the argument, as he describes the Greek use of mythology: "At best, it is but Fancy, or the aggregating Faculty of the mind – not Imagination, or the modifying, and co-adunating Faculty." The thoughtful phrasing suggests that it is probably not the first occasion of its being used; in any case it comes out still more strongly a year or two later in a commendation of Wordsworth in a letter to Richard Sharp:

Wordsworth is a Poet, a most original Poet – he no more resembles Milton than Milton resembles Shakespere – no more resembles Shakespere than Shakespere resembles Milton – he is himself: and I dare affirm that he will hereafter be admitted as the first & greatest philosophical Poet – the only man who has effected a compleat and constant synthesis of Thought & Feeling and combined them with Poetic Forms, with the music of pleasurable passion and with Imagination or the *modifying* Power in that highest sense of the word in which I have ventured to oppose it to Fancy, or the *aggregating* power – in that sense in which it is a dim Analogue of Creation, not all that we can *believe* but all that we can *conceive* of creation. (15 December 1804; *CL* 2: 1034)

In this statement a suggestion that had been shadowed in the passage about the Hebrew poets emerges more clearly into the light of day: when we contemplate Imagination, viewed as the modifying power, we are glimpsing something of the processes involved in the Divine creation itself. We also understand something of what Lamb meant when he spoke of Coleridge and "his god, Wordsworth."[6]

Now, however, a fissure was to open out in the latter relationship, corresponding to a suspicion on Coleridge's part that in his human relationships at least his god might have feet of clay. As that suspicion grew, and as his unfulfilled relationship with Sara Hutchinson became more painful, the element of revelation in nature dropped away. Simultaneously his impulse to poetry gave way to a concern with literary criticism. But as this happened an observation from an earlier place proved still to be a germinal element. He had ascribed the power to pass out of oneself as being one which had perhaps been achieved only by Shakespeare. Now Shakespeare assumed the centre of the stage as the poet to whom he most wished to give his attention.

This new prominence of Shakespeare, particularly in Coleridge's thinking concerning the creative imagination, is evident from a long note on *Venus and Adonis* which appears in one of his notebooks (probably in preparation for a lecture of 1808) and in which one can see his view developing towards the account of Shakespeare which was eventually to appear in *Biographia Literaria*:

1. Sense of Beauty – this thro' the whole poem, even to almost effeminacy of sweetness – good sign/ painter who begins with old men's and old women's faces, a bad sign – coarse & strong is easily done so as to *strike* –

2. With things remote from his own feelings – and in which the romanticity gives a vividness to the naturalness of the sentiments & feelings –

3. Love of natural Objects – quote the Hare, p.23 – there is indeed a far more admirable description precedent, but less fitted for public recitation/

4. Fancy, or the aggregative Power – 13th. p[age] – Full gently now &c – the bringing together Images dissimilar in the main by some one point or more of Likeness – distinguished – read from Pocket book – / both common in the writers of Shakspere's time/

5. – That power of & energy of what a living poet has grandly & appropriately. To flash upon that inward Eye Which is the Bliss of Solitude – & to make every thing present by a Series of Images – This an absolute Essential of Poetry, & of itself would form a poet, tho' not of the highest Class – It is however a most hopeful

Symptom, & the V[enus] & A[donis] is one continued Specimen/
6. Imagination/ power of modifying one image or feeling by the precedent or following ones – . – So often after afterwards to be illustrated that at present I shall speak only of – one of its effects – namely, that of combining many circumstances into one moment of thought to produce that ultimate end of human Thought, and human Feeling, Unity and thereby the reduction of the Spirit to its Principle & Fountain, who alone is truly *one*. (Quote the passage p. 28. *before this* observation.) – & p.29. – for
7. <The describing natural objects by cloathing them appropriately with human passions/ Lo, here the gentle Lark/>
8. Energy, depth, and activity of Thought without which a man may be a pleasing and affecting Poet; but never a great one. Here introduce Dennis's – enthus[iasm]: & vulgar pass[ion]: – & from the excess of this in Shakespere be grateful that circumstances probably originating in choice led him to the Drama, the subject of my next lecture – & end with Chapman's – (*CN* 3: 3247)

For several years after this his chief critical – and indeed literary – activity was the giving of lectures, some of which are of absorbing interest, particularly in terms of the long engagement with Shakespeare that is indicated here. Important and illuminating comments on Shakespeare sprang from a development of Johnson's view of him as a poet of nature, the sphere of his activity being extended to that element of nature that is to be found in the human consciousness. A further important factor was the emergence of a criticism relating to the role of imagination and the workings of the "one Life." Throughout the period, as Coleridge had been working on his view of literary criticism, A.W. Schlegel had been developing his own positions in successive lecture courses given in different European universities, thus giving the romantic movement in Germany its intellectual basis. An important element in his contribution had been to bring the concept of organic life into the centre of the discussion. Coleridge's interest in what he had to say was, however, modified by the fact that his criticism had already been affected deeply by his own concept of "the one Life," which was in many ways a good deal more subtle. Whereas the German critics thought of the organic basically in terms of the growth of organic form, their basic image being that of a vegetable, unfolding itself according to the inward idea that already existed in its seed, Coleridge's view went further. Organic life was also characterised by the play of energy: if one were thinking of art in those terms, therefore, one should think in terms of energies as well as forms. Nor were those energies to be treated as a simple phenomenon, since they had passive as well as active modes – a fact which applied also to the responding mind. Finally, following the intuition already mentioned, he believed that if the mind was allowed to submit itself in passivity not to the external world but to its own powers it would discover in its own depths a secret creativity which would reveal something of the creative power of the divine. This, one of his main keys for unlocking Shakespeare's mastery, was at once his masterstroke and his weak point, for the theological tradition of the society in which he found himself was always likely to reject, as a kind of overweening arrogance, too ready an identification between creative mind and creative divinity.

The comprehensiveness and subtlety of Coleridge's thinking and its vulnerability are equally apparent. On the one hand he had produced a form of organic thinking which was intricate in its approach, allowing for both passive and active energies. In the process of doing so he had given it a beguilingly human reference by binding it back to basic activities such as the indrawing and expelling of air in the act of breathing or the systole and diastole inherent in every heartbeat or the necessary interweaving of waking and sleep. And at the same time this whole process could still be drawn into one and made revelatory of the whole divine process.

Yet in more sober moments this might appear a grand fantasy rather than a system by which human beings could hope to live; and this was particularly likely to be the case when he went on to bring the whole process back into the Christian tradition. In his own states of guilt, for that matter, identification of the artistic process with the being of God could appear blasphemous. The whole remained an engaging concatenation of ideas, strangely compelling in its hints of answers to many basic human needs.

It is against the background of this thinking that Coleridge's quarrel with Wordsworth in 1810 must be considered. For it had been an essential element in the development of this thinking that Wordsworth at least believed in what he was doing; and Coleridge must also have noticed how much of the thinking in *The Prelude* drew on similar patterns of ideas. Yet in now saying that he had no hope of him Wordsworth appeared to be disowning the enterprise. The quarrel was patched up; but it was followed by other wounding blows when Wordsworth produced the 1815 edition of his poems, where he saw fit to add a preface in which the Imagination was described as the power which "draws all things to one" and the view ascribed to one of his "more esteemed friends" – the "friend" being not, as one might have expected, Coleridge but Charles Lamb (*WPrW* 3: 34). In his supplementary essay, similarly, he paid tribute to the Germans for having awakened his own countrymen to the understanding of Shakespeare (*WPrW* 3: 69), making no reference to the fact that Coleridge had spent the past seven years trying to do just that. It was this slighting of his achievements which, I believe, drew Coleridge to the conclusion that he must express his own view – and in the process try to get to the bottom of differences between himself and his old friend which he had sensed as long ago as 1802. So it was that a projected preliminary essay to the new edition of his own poems turned first into an "Autobiographia literaria" and then into *Biographia Literaria*.[7]

Before he could grapple with the matters implicit in Wordsworth's essay, however, he must try once and for all to tease out his own views on the question of the Imagination. Yet he was well aware that it was hard to do this without risking the impression of setting forth a pantheistic view. So he found himself driven to the desperate expedient of appropriating, with a little rewriting, large chunks of Schelling on the subject, and then cutting across the whole problem by reporting the receipt of a letter (written, he later acknowledged, entirely by himself[8]), dissuading him from continuing the enterprise and advising him to save the subject for another work. He then moved into a gnomic vein, setting down his own version of the Imagination in a number of pregnant sentences which have been the subject of critical debate ever since:

> The IMAGINATION then, I consider either as primary, or as secondary. The primary IMAGINATION I hold to be the living Power and prime Agent of all human Perception, and as a repetition in the finite mind of the eternal act of creation in the infinite I AM. The secondary Imagination I consider as an echo of the former, co-existing with the conscious will, yet still as identical with the primary in the *kind* of its agency, and differing only in *degree*, and in the *mode* of its operation. It dissolves, diffuses, dissipates, in order to recreate; or where this process is rendered impossible, yet still at all events it struggles to idealize and to unify. It is essentially *vital*, even as all objects (*as* objects) are essentially fixed and dead.
>
> FANCY, on the contrary, has no other counters to play with, but fixities and definites. The Fancy is indeed no other than a mode of Memory emancipated from the order of time and space; while it is blended with, and modified by that empirical phenomenon of the will, which we express by the word CHOICE. But equally with the ordinary memory the Fancy must receive all its materials ready made from the law of association. (*BL* 1: 304–5)

These paragraphs have probably engendered more discussion among critics than any others that Coleridge wrote. They have been defended and praised as a kind of bedrock upon which a defence of the role of the imagination can be mounted; they have also – and more often, perhaps – been attacked as offering a distinction without substance. Many have confessed themselves baffled by the attempt to separate two powers, imagination and fancy, which strike them as more or less synonymous, and have found themselves still more bewildered when the imagination itself is divided into two further areas, of which the "secondary" seems to correspond most recognisably with what many artists would normally think that they are trying to do.

The very terms in which these distinctions are presented – "like those of a royal proclamation," Hugh Sykes Davies once said – assist the sense that Coleridge's categories are presented as if they were a kind of last judgment on literature. Discussion of the passage has not been helped, moreover, by the fact that many critics have followed I.A. Richards in taking the phrase "the living Power and prime Agent of all human Perception" to mean something very homely:

> The Primary Imagination is normal perception that produces the usual world of the senses,
>> That inanimate cold world allowed
>> To the poor loveless ever-anxious crowd
>
> the world of motor-buses, beef-steaks, and acquaintances, the framework of things and events within which we maintain our everyday existence, the world of the routine satisfaction of our minimum exigences.[9]

If we read the account of Primary Imagination simply in these terms we shall indeed have some difficulty in seeing how it can be distinguished from the Fancy. And Coleridge cannot altogether be exempted from responsibility for such a reading. But the formulations make more sense if they are considered not as isolated dicta but as marking a staging-point in the long discussion which Coleridge was carrying out concerning the role of the mind itself in relation to nature. Coleridge indeed makes the secondary Imagination the active and vital power, but as we have seen it was crucial to his view of the matter that the energies of the mind were both active and passive in their operation. If the imagination allowed itself to become simply passive to the external world ("the world of motorbuses, beef-steaks and acquaintances") it would indeed enter the realm of Fancy, where it would have nothing to play with but the dead counters of objects; if on the other hand it was attentive to its own subconscious powers it would find itself in correspondence with the true sources of creativity. When Coleridge speaks of the primary imagination as the "prime Agent of all human perception" he may well be alluding to the fact that every act of perception contains a creative element: but his more important reference is to the level of creative activity at which the artist allows the shaping power of imagination to take over. At that point, he believes, the artist is in touch with the creative powers of the divine – repeating in the finite mind "the eternal act of creation in the infinite I AM." And this is for him only an example – albeit the most striking one – of the way in which the inward being of the individual is always capable of being linked to that of the divine.

Once he has set forward this cryptic formulation Coleridge can feel free to allow it to be the one by which he judges Wordsworth's achievement, suggesting where he fulfils it and where he falls short. But he can also continue to explore the question of the subconscious powers themselves, as in the great chapter on metre; and then to end the whole book with an adoring contemplation of the "I AM" "whose choral echo is the universe" (*BL* 2: 247–8).

It was suggested earlier that as Coleridge's most compressed statements of the years up to 1808 are examined one can detect in many of them a germinal point which will find fuller expression in the next. But there is also a larger process at work, foreshadowed as early as in "The Eolian Harp," by which the poet feels the whole of that creative process to be under judgment from the divine; and that too is an ineradicable feature of his work. After his spiritual crisis of 1813 he found himself in a state of guilt, needing to invoke the divine mercy. Despite the creative burst which enabled him to complete *Biographia Literaria* this is true of his later dealings with that work also, so that some years later, according to Sara Coleridge, he even went so far as to strike out the passage about the "infinite I AM" in one copy.[10] For the same reason his critical powers were turned increasingly to religious questions and to the Bible. The development is by no means to be disprized: it turns on Coleridge's desire to find a way of keeping faith with the past, a question, the question of fidelity, to which criticism has not addressed itself very much. He praised the novels of Sir Walter Scott, for example, on the grounds that

> the contest between the Loyalists and their opponents can never be absolute, for it is the contest between the two great moving Principles of social Humanity – religious adherence to the Past and the Ancient, the Desire and the admiration of Permanence, on the one hand; and the Passion for increase of Knowledge, for Truth as the offspring of Reason, in short, the mighty Instincts of Progression and Free-agency on the other. (Letter to Allsop; 8 April 1820: *CL* 5: 35)

As critics we are likely to address ourselves most readily to the progressive element in Coleridge, and particularly to his examination of the play of energies in the human psyche. The idea that creativity can involve both active and passive states of mind is one that can be explored irrespective of one's beliefs about the human relationship to the divine. But the fact that Coleridge should also have felt himself to be under judgment does not, in the end, mark a weakness in his critical position. It may have inhibited him from developing some of his critical insights to the extent that some of his readers would like, but it also showed another aspect of his awareness – that of his existence as a human being in a universe that was in the end, riddling and mysterious. That awareness (there all his life, and presented most dramatically in *The Ancient Mariner*) inhabited his critical sense also, giving it another dimension of discourse to run with and against the others.

JOHN BEER

NOTES

1. See *CN* I: 1070 and 3: 3285; *BL* Chapter 15; 2:19, 19n citing Naucratius as reported in Cave's *History*.
2. The scope of theorising that was possible has recently been well indicated by Ian Wylie in *Young Coleridge and the Philosophers of Nature* (Oxford: Clarendon P., 1989).
3. See the letter to Sotheby quoted above, 9, 10 Sept. 1802 (*CL* 2: 864, 866). For the possible use in Germany see, Clement Carlyon, *Early Years and Late Reflections* (London: Whittaker, 1836–58), 4 vols: 1: 193, where it appears as "the concentrated definition of Spinoza"; although this is presented in the context of Coleridge's stay in Germany, the following pages, with their reference to Giordano Bruno, make it rather more likely that Coleridge gave it to Carlyon at a later meeting in London, probably in 1803.
4. *CN* 1: 787; *WPW* 1: 148. See Coleridge's comment (*CL* 2: 811): "the first passages were indeed partly taken from notes of mine."
5. Preface to the first edition of 1816: *PW* 1: 215.
6. Letter to Manning, 5 April 1880; *The Letters of Charles and Mary Lamb*, ed. E. Marrs (Ithaca and London: Cornell U.P., 1975–76), 3 vols; 1: 191.
7. See Editors' Introduction to *BL*. A more concise account may be found in *CL* 4: 578–9, 578n–9n.
8. See *BL* 1: lvii, citing a letter to Curtis, *CL* 4: 728.
9. I.A. Richards, *Coleridge on Imagination* (London: Kegan Paul & Co., 1934; [revised Bloomington, 1950]), 58.
10. See *Biographia Literaria*, ed. H.N. Coleridge and Sara Coleridge (London, 1847), 2 vols. 1: 297n.

Coleridge's Notebook Scribblings

Rhetoric, that art of persuasive speaking or writing, is an old subject. Indeed, it had seemed for a time to be old in the most pejorative, rather than venerative, sense of the word: worn-out, tired, pedantic and even boring. In recent years, rhetoric has come to the forefront of attention, though no doubt for many poets, politicians, a few literary critics, and some others, there has never been any doubt of its centrality, not only in coping with life, but in understanding literature. The romantic rejection, not of rhetoric itself, but only of the terminological disputes and hairsplittings of eighteenth-century neo-classicism, culminated in Croce's and in Spingarn's abandoning the old classical methods for "intuition and expression." Beginning with I.A. Richards, with the New Criticism of Ransom, Tate, Brooks, and Empson, and with Frye, a revival of interest in a less pedantic, less classificatory science of rhetoric emerged, culminating in post-structural developments. Derrida, Paul de Man, and others have certainly also contributed to restoring the study of rhetoric to a central position, taking their cue from Nietzsche perhaps, in rejecting the old distinction between logic (and also oratory) and rhetoric as untenable. Taking up the Ciceronian tradition, they argued that logic and grammar (the "invention" and arrangements of material) cannot be separated from style (or rhetoric, in the narrow sense of the word as eloquence and use of figures of speech). As Coleridge might have argued, there may be a distinction, but there can be no division, between logic (or grammar) and rhetoric, between, that is, material arrangement and style.

Shelley, elaborating Coleridge's insights into the symbol, went on to argue in the *Defence of Poetry* that language itself is essentially rhetorical. He thereby rejected eighteenth-century language theorists' notions of a logical base or essence of language, with a veneer of ornamentation or rhetoric overlaying it, thus establishing an alleged distinction between the logical language of science and the emotional, pleasurable language of poetry, which Shelley abhorred. Since for Shelley language is essentially metaphorical, and not strictly logical, logic was merely a systematising of familiar, conventional metaphors. As such, logic and reason were not conducive to new truths. Poetry and imagination, not science or logic, are the means of expressing and discovering new truths about human experience and the universe.

For the Greeks, rhetoric was inextricably involved with ethics and the Good (in theory, if not in practice: see Plato's complaints, in the *Meno* and elsewhere, about the abuse of the art of persuasion by the Sophists and others). Moreover, the truly Good was of course inseparable from the Beautiful; one aim of rhetoric was always, as a consequence, to lead to the ethical through the pleasure derived from the beautiful in art and language. This connection between ethics and rhetoric was the origin of notions about poetry as necessarily didactic, and not merely pleasurable, as, for example, Horace argued. Coleridge contributed to this continuing debate by insisting that delight and pleasure are the surest means of instruction, thus refusing, like Blake before him, to allow the distinction between truth and pleasure to become a division. Not surprisingly, Coleridge also argued against an absolute division between poetry and prose (a distinction originating in part in the old classical dualism of poetry and oratory). In his well-known rejection of Wordsworth's incautious statement that poetry differs from prose only in its having distinct metre and rhyme, Coleridge argued that metre and rhyme fundamentally affect form and language. Hence, the quality of the language of poetry differs in kind from that of prose. Yet, he also rejected any easy division of poetic language from prose on the basis of versification, adopting the traditional, classical view (of Cicero, Quintilian, and others), that Plato, Xenophon, and the Bible, for example, though not verse, were poetry of the highest kind.

The art and study of rhetoric, whether in philosophy, politics, or literature, involved, then, the teaching of (logical or grammatical) skills of selection and organisation of material, and the (rhetorical) skills of elaboration and embellishment, through figures of speech and tone. "Metadiscourse," that classical gesture of shifting attention from what is being said, either, first, to the fact that it is being said, or, second, to how something is being said, has always been a major traditional, rhetorical, conscious device, in poetry, narrative, and non-fiction, since Western literature began. A related but distinct technique, what in classical rhetorical theory was called "hypotyposis," involves the bringing to life of issues discussed, the mimicking of acts, and the lively presentation of processes of speech, thinking, and even writing itself. It is inextricably involved in the complex notion of "mimesis," meaning, in part, the identification of members of the audience with the characters and the narrator of a poem. "Mimesis" insists that the role of the audience is that of a vitally active participant, rather than a passive observer. Plato's correction of the popular theory of mimesis involved his demand that an emotional identification be either followed or replaced by a rational, reflective self-consciousness of one's acts of reading and responding. He called this the "true mimesis." In Quintilian terms, as for Cicero, hypotyposis and mimesis involved not merely telling or stating something *via* propositional statements, but also bringing it to life by showing or demonstrating the idea stated.[1] Metadiscursive devices are a primary means of achieving hypotyposis. They include such obvious ones as "what I mean is," "of course," "the point is that," along with the less obvious and more profound narrative devices which seek to justify, emphasise or to foreground both earlier assertions, rhetorical strategies, and language itself. Such classical devices constitute what we often call today "writing about writing," "self-conscious authorial intrusions," and "poetry about poetry," for example. Short metadiscursive parenthetical expressions, along with the other more elaborate devices, function to focus speech or writing on language itself (as such recent writers as Roman Jakobsen have repeatedly shown), while, analogously, narrative focuses on the act of story-telling. These apparent "digressions" (the rhetoric) from the main line of argument (the logic), these gestures of calling attention to the fact or way of making statements or telling the reader things, are a way of shifting attention from content or ideas to the living drama of thinking, according to classical rhetorical theory. As Coleridge recognised, through intelligent rhetoric, an author can convey to the reader lively, immediate impressions of a mind in the act of thinking, a mind vividly struggling with language to formulate relations into articulate being. The ideas in question are thereby made more immediately present to the reader, and hence become more comprehensible and persuasive.

Rhetoric, then, can be used in the service of greater understanding, not merely in a "striving after effects." For Plato, Longinus, Cicero, Quintilian, Bacon, Coleridge, and Hazlitt, to name a few, hypotyposis was intimately tied up with these metadiscursive strategies: hence, the mimicking of thinking, of the struggling for linguistic expression and verbal felicity, was far more important than the presentation of dogmas and opinions. The goal for these writers was not so much to convey finished arguments as to communicate the nature of the process of thinking by enlivening it, by demonstrating it for the reader or listener in the very language. This Platonic, Ciceronian, Quintilian tradition of emphasis upon demonstration and enlivening presentation versus mere telling or recounting of past events, arising out of their efforts to develop a science of poetics and rhetoric, was vigorously taken up and revitalised by Blake, Coleridge, Shelley, and others, both in poetry, prose, and in theorising about language and poetry. An explicit and systematic appreciation of the importance of hypotyposis and metadiscourse has reappeared in modern times in formalist, new-critical, structural, and post-structural criticism, in varying guises and degrees of lucidity, due in part to the emphasis overtly placed on it by Henry James, Conrad, and many Modernist writers like Dorothy Richardson, Djuna Barnes, and others.

COLERIDGE'S CLASSICAL STRATEGIES

There is, we can conclude, little new in modern notions about metadiscourse or hypotyposis – poetry about poetry, self-conscious language, narrative about story-telling, reading-situation analogies. All can be found in literature from Homer, through Plato, in ancient Sanskrit drama,[2] in the theorising of Cicero and Quintilian, through to Chaucer, Shakespeare, the English and German Romantics and so on, up to our own era. The notion that these strategies and ideas are peculiar to our own modern ways of thinking is puzzling to anyone with even a bare familiarity with the history of Western literature and criticism. Perhaps we become too hypnotised by our particular terminology and jargon to see its intrinsic similarity to earlier modes of expression. Whatever the reason for this predilection to believe our own ways of perceiving literature new, we can certainly see metadiscourse and hypotyposis operating relentlessly in Coleridge's prose, as well as in his poetry. Whether in notebooks, letters, or marginalia, or whether in "finished," polished, published writings, we find him constantly resorting to these ancient, classical, rhetorical devices, to such an extent that his "digressions" often become his main argument, his "metadiscourse" his primary discourse, and his hypotyposis the substance of his communicative efforts. Substance becomes shadow, and shadow substance, as Coleridge seeks to teach not what to think, feel or imagine, but how to engage in genuine thinking, feeling or imagining. He seeks to communicate the nature of thinking itself in the hopes of stimulating his readers from the position of passive observer to "fellow labourer," from consumer of others' ideas and opinions to active formulator of one's own thoughts. Critics often respond to this assertion by arguing that surely Plato, Aristotle, Kant, Hegel, Berkeley, Coleridge, and so on, were saying something more than just this; surely they were seeking to convey something more than merely how to think, than merely to teach their readers the nature and character of thought. Were genuine thinking (as opposed to the mindless absorption and adoption of others' thoughts) a little less out of the ordinary, this criticism might carry some weight.

According to the classical tradition of the science of rhetoric, poetry, and/or oratory, there can exist a powerful appeal in an awkward, apparently spontaneous style, as opposed to the power of a polished, carefully turned artfulness. This ethical appeal arises from the association of artifice with deceit, and of honesty with directness, spontaneity, and artlessness. The appearance of private and frank, open deliberations suggests an unconsciousness of any audience and, therefore, a freedom from efforts to persuade or deceive so much as to express one's true thoughts sincerely. Curiously, this notion of overt audience-awareness was used in classical rhetoric to distinguish the orator from the poet, and was taken up with a vengeance by the Romantics, and later by J.S. Mill. According to them, the poet sang in solitude, and was not "heard," so much as "overheard." This claim is in itself, of course, a rhetorical strategy: the romantic pretence to innocent, artless, unpremeditated outpourings was hardly naive sentimentalising. The reader/critic who took it literally would have had to have been inordinately ignorant of the traditional, classical lore and literary conventions familiar to poets and readers of the eighteenth century. The strategy was an open, publicly well-known one; but nevertheless, it had its effect: that ethical appeal of sincerity and truth.

In one sense, this strategy was closely related to the Romantic rejection of much eighteenth-century neo-classical artfulness, which had in some cases been carried so far as to be no art but mere artifice: ornamentation for its own sake, and a mark of "false" poetry. Thus the idea of poetry itself, what it was, what it ought to be, was at stake, while matters of taste and decorum underwent a quite remarkable revolution. Coleridge never fell into the trap of oversimplifying this transition as a "back to nature" movement, as he feared Wordsworth had at times done. Coleridge was all too familiar with literary conventions and strategies not to recognise this as yet another kind of artistic device. He did seek, however, to articulate more precisely what distinguished art from artifice. His conclusion was certainly not that "art" was, literally, free from artfulness. It was in the imaginative coincidence of matter and manner (these only distinctions, of course, not separate things), and in that resulting unity of ideas with form, that Coleridge believed art to be distinct from mere artifice. This was not merely a version of decorum, either, since Coleridge believed that matter shapes itself from within, according to the laws of the imagination. Coincidence of matter and manner involved, consequently, not a merely fancifully appropriate ornamentation of already conceived ideas ("decorum" in its undebased meaning carried with it some of these Coleridgean profundities).

The "manner" of Coleridge's "occasional" jottings (marginalia and notebooks, and sometimes – only sometimes – his letters) is certainly distinct from that of his published writings. But in both, he draws on his quite phenomenal knowledge of the literary and critical tradition before him, and on the philosophical and theoretical tradition from classical and medieval to Renaissance and "modern" (to him, at least) writings. Not only the matter, but the manner of his writings, whether occasional or published, is saturated with evidence of this appreciation of the debates about rhetoric and logic, poetry and oratory, and so on, which took so many varied forms throughout Western history. Our understanding of Coleridge's (and any writer's) achievements will be limited markedly by the extent of our own familiarity with the literary history in which he was as deeply immersed as any writer of his time. The knowledge that the tradition was steeped in an awareness of metadiscursive strategies, of hypotyposis, and of virtually every other technique that our modern writing thinks it has "discovered," is almost a precondition for reading intelligently today.

As is widely recognised, Coleridge's private jottings are no less rhetorical and strategy-laden than his public, published writings or lectures were. They are certainly different in their strategies, but no less "literary" or interesting for that difference. Indeed, they offer precisely that "ethical" appeal that the Ciceronian–Quintilian tradition recognised in certain types of apparently "awkward," unadorned styles, with their appearance of private, spontaneous expression. The assumption that the style of Coleridge's published works (sections of which are often reworked versions of private jottings) are superior in "literary" quality or polish to the "original" formulations in notebooks or letters or marginalia, that the notebook "style," for example, is inferior, has long since gone out of fashion (however much it may persist unconsciously). This is in part due to the recognition that the unpolished style accomplished precisely what the classical theories of rhetoric accounted some of the higher arts, namely hypotyposis and metadiscourse. Awkwardness is often only apparently awkward, moreover: awkwardness can be artfulness for a specific purpose, such as the ethical appeal of greater sincerity. The poet pretends to be overheard, rather than heard, since a proclaimed consciousness of an audience suggests dissimulation; whereas arguably the greater dissimulation resides in the pretence to unconsciousness of any audience, an open strategy that the Romantics adopted in order to break out of the artificial constraints of neo-classicism. But to be taken literally by their reader – ? When the poet singing in solitude was a familiar metaphor itself precisely for art versus artifice, poetry versus oratory?

"SELF-CIRCLING ENERGIES"

The comments made in this section on reading Coleridge's notebooks are hardly going to strike a reader as new. But they may at least provide some arresting examples which will add to the interesting insights of other Coleridgeans on this topic, primarily by comparing short passages from, for example, *Biographia Literaria*, *The Friend*, and *Church and State* with related notebook entries. The comparisons made below will be guided by the context of the classical tradition of rhetoric provided above, particularly with references to hypotyposis, metadiscourse, logic versus rhetoric, and the question of ethics and rhetoric. Issues about the distinction between poetry and prose, the meaning of "poetic-prose," Shelley's notion of language as essentially metaphorical (with the resulting breakdown of the notion that logic is the language of truth and rhetoric that of passion), the relation of the audience to the text, the nature of reading and interpretation, and questions about specific rhetorical devices will be touched upon. While much is gained in terms of polish and completeness in the published works, it has been, in part correctly I think, noted by others that something of the "living drama of thought" (that hypotyposis) is on many occasions lost. An awareness of Coleridge's adaptation of classical rhetorical skills in both private and published writings, however, enormously increases our appreciation of his art. It is well to keep in mind, though, that like "irony," "hypotyposis" is often poorly understood; indeed, even the largest implications of the related concept "metadiscourse," are often overlooked. In all three cases, it is here argued (as in much modern theory) that Coleridge's (perfectly classical) notion of the "reader as fellow labourer" is not to be underestimated or interpreted too superficially.

These issues go to the heart of what is involved in aesthetic experience

– of what art, poetry, and audience response are by their very nature. The best classical examples of the "reach" of these concepts are the theories of mimesis and Plato's exemplary Socratic dialogues: Socrates' aim is to draw his companion into active participation. Plato's aim is, analogously, to draw the reader into active participation. But (and here Plato departs from the popular theory of mimesis to offer his "true imitation"), the participation is of such a kind as to scrutinise both the companion's thoughts and opinions as well as, through irony, metaphor, framework techniques, hypotyposis, and metadiscourse (amongst other rhetorical strategies), those notions, beliefs, and values of the reader. The *Meno*, with its exemplary "dialogue within a dialogue" (the slave-boy "demonstration"), is an excellent reminder of how prevalent these self-conscious narrative techniques were in Greek literature.[3] Sophocles' *Oedipus Rex* is another good example, where self-knowledge and self-consciousness is the central theme, not merely for Oedipus, but for each member of the Athenian, and later, other audience. As Vernant has pointed out, the Greek tragedians were putting the Athenian audience on the stage not merely for mindless emotional identification, but for reflective self-examination, in order to display to them their own prejudices, notions and values, in order to force them to examine and reassess those values and prejudices.[4] These tragedies have not lost their force for putting the modern audience on the stage, for precisely the same purpose, namely, self-awareness through self-knowledge. Sophoclean irony "breaks through the boundary of the work of art" to include the reader and implicate her. Far from being merely a matter of verbal or dramatic irony, Sophocles' irony goes to the very structural heart of the "drama" of reading and response. As the German ironists would put it, the reader-audience becomes one of the participants in the work not only at an emotional level of mimetic identification, but also at an intellectual, reflective level of self-conscious scrutiny of that emotional identification. Thus, reader and audience responses and reactions (interpretations) are a covert, metaphorical and ironic sub-text. As the author of that seminal work, *Art as Experience*, wrote, the "spectator theory" of knowledge and art is debunked.[5] The alert audience can no longer sustain the myth of being outside the world of the text, looking down on it from above and observing it detached. Nor can the audience naively identify emotionally, as some mimetic theories would have it. As readers, we are in the text and of it, while one of the central qualities of aesthetic experience is the awakening to the (often shocking and unwanted) true mimesis of Plato, namely the awareness or self-consciousness that one's own processes of reading, perception, and interpretation are anticipated, portrayed, recognised, and frequently "deconstructed." The act of interpretation and reading is at issue centrally and thematically, not merely secondarily and supplementarily to the meaning of the text.

The several paired passages quoted below from notebooks and

published works illustrate Coleridge's rhetorical skills in dramatically drawing the reader not just emotionally, but reflectively into the expanding web of the text. Let us first take the following passages:

> I (a) Mackintosh intertrudes, not introduces his beauties. Nothing grows out of his main argument but much is shoved between – each digression occasions a move backward to find the road again – like a sick man he recoils after every affection. The Serpent by which the ancients emblem'd the Inventive faculty appears to me, in its mode of motion most exactly to emblem a writer of Genius. He varies his course yet still glides onwards – all lines of motion are his – all beautiful, and all propulsive – ... So varied he & of his tortuous train/ Curls many a wanton wreath; yet still he proceeds & is proceeding. – (*CN* I: 609)
>
> (b) Even the most mobile of creatures, the serpent, makes a rest of its own body, and drawing up its voluminous train from behind on this fulcrum, propels itself onward. On the other hand, it is a proverb in all languages, that (relatively to man at least) what would stand still must retrograde. (*C&S* 24)
>
> (c) The reader should be carried forward, not merely or chiefly by the mechanical impulse of curiosity, or by a restless desire to arrive at the final solution; but by the pleasurable activity of mind excited by the attractions of the journey itself. Like the motion of a serpent, which the Egyptians made the emblem of intellectual power; or like the path of sound through the air; at every step he pauses and half recedes, and from the retrogressive movement collects the force which again carries him onward. (*BLS* 2: 11)

It might first be noted that these three passages occur in contexts concerning issues about the nature of poetry, part–whole relations and unity, the philosophical issue dear to Coleridge's heart about the distinction between opposites and contraries, and the matter of the use, abuse, and invention of new words. (These passages are also closely related to passages quoted below.) It is also notable that neither the editors of the notebooks nor the editors of the new editions of *Biographia* and *Church and State* saw any need to cross-reference these three passages. This peculiar omission may suggest that readers and critics alike are not giving Coleridge's rhetorical strategies the attention they warrant, seeing them as mere ornaments rather than as central to his methods. Moreover, it also suggests that we may still be reading Coleridge in too "prosaic" a way; reading his prose, that is, as if it were merely discursive and logical argumentation, rather than rhetorical and poetic in substantive, irreducible ways. Shelley's "Defence of Poetry" has, clearly, suffered from the same misreading, as has other "prose." We would learn more from such prose if we gave it the same attention that we give to some poetry. A disquisition proceeding via argument, familiar propositional logic, and discursive narrative is hardly, indeed not even remotely, a just description of the style of writing of the *Biographia* or the "Defence." Such texts are better read not as proceeding essentially linearly, but as proceeding essentially via metaphor, imagery, allusion, hypotyposis, and so on; like the movement of the serpent, these texts vary their course, yet still glide onward, at every step pausing and half receding, collecting the force which again propels the narrative forward. "Digressions," extended metaphors, footnotes, examples, and imagery are means of pausing in order to provide force for forward movement. They are not incidental to the text, but essential moments of it; they are the very means by which a fulcrum for propulsion is brought into the narrative. We profit most from such texts if we read them as we listen to music, not mistaking the fact that while one note follows another, we must nevertheless gather up the notes and phrases into larger, imaginatively complex structures, so that we actually "hear" the music, as opposed merely to listening to it. The serpent metaphor is not an unapt emblem for such writing, as well as for imaginative reading. Circle and spiral metaphors, so beloved by Shelley (as in his prolific use of radial imagery such as star, flower, and song), are repeatedly invoked, and are the heart of the imagery and structuring principles of these texts.

If we look closely at these passages, we see that extended metaphor is Coleridge's primary means of hypotyposis – of bringing alive for the reader, of demonstrating as well as stating ideas. When "polishing" for publication, more explicitly metadiscursive devices tend to be introduced ("the reader should be carried forward ..."), which back up the hypotyposis/metaphorical strategy, thus alerting the reader to the fact that Coleridge is drawing her attention to reading, writing, perception, and interpretation as a covert, and at times, explicit subject matter (see below passages VIII). In the notebook entry, the serpent's motion is likened to that of the "Writer of Genius"; in the *Biographia*, it has become a metaphor for the reader's method of reading (suggesting that the two are not entirely different types of intellectual activity), while in *Church and State* it is used as an example of the distinction between contraries and opposites, specifically, the relation of permanence to change. As an illustration of the sheer power of thought articulating itself into language, the notebook passage strikes one as markedly superior to the other more finely finished texts. That "awkwardness" of style, that jerky, unconventionally punctuated string of phrases (and how significant a role that departure from conventional punctuation plays!) forces the reader into a far more imaginative perception than the smoothly flowing, decorous, and "proper" style of the two published versions. The notebook entry is virtually self-illustrative; the first two sentences do what they describe: they "intrude," "shove" sections in between, "recoil," and digress "backwardly," but deliberately, and for the rhetorical effect of hypotyposis. By contrast, the second two sentences "vary their course, yet still glide onwards – all lines of motion are his – all beautiful, & all propulsive –." Here, Coleridge strikingly "illustrates," by opposite styles, what he is arguing, as well as introducing a metaphor involving the larger issue of the nature of his style throughout the *Biographia*, the style also of much poetic prose. Amongst all the digressions, asides, examples, metaphors, and other miscellaneous miscellany, Coleridge "proceeds & is proceeding," as we can discover, if we take account of the classical rhetorical techniques that keep the text whole and in motion, moving ever forward, guided and unified by its central concern for the nature of imagination itself – that is, of imaginative thinking.

The passages quoted below further illustrate Coleridge's fascination with the serpent-like, self-circling motion of that "self-circling energy," imagination:

> II (a) Let us consider what we do when we leap. We first resist the gravitating power by an act purely voluntary, and then by another act, voluntary in part, we yield to it in order to light on the spot, which we had previously proposed to ourselves. Now let a man watch his mind while he is composing; or, to take a still more common case, while he is trying to recollect a name; and he will find the process completely analogous. Most of my readers will have observed a small water insect on the surface of rivulets, which throws a cinque spotted shadow fringed with prismatic colours on the sunny bottom of the brook; and will have noticed, how the little animal wins its way up against the stream, by alernate pulses of active and passive motion, now resisting the current, and now yielding to it in order to gather strength and a momentary fulcrum for a further propulsion. This is no unapt emblem of the mind's self-experience in the act of thinking. (*BLS* 1: 85–6)
>
> (b) I had been talking of the association of Ideas, and endeavoring to convince an Idolater of Hume & Hartley, that this was strictly speaking a law only of the memory & imagination, of the Stuff out of which we make our conceptions & perceptions, not of the thinking faculty, by which we make them – that it was as the +power+ force of gravitation to leaping to any given point – without gravitation this would be impossible, and yet equally impossible to leap except by a power counteracting first, and then using the force of gravitation. That Will, strictly synonimous with the individualizing Principle, the "I" of every rational Being, was this governing and applying Power – (*CN* 3: 3708; and see *CN* 3: 4015, for a fascinating example)

Note the preponderance of strictly metadiscursive rhetoric in the published version (a): "Let us consider ..." and "Most of my readers ...," while, crowning the passage, we read, "This is no unapt emblem of the mind's self-experiencing in the act of thinking." Here, the inclusion of the water-insect extended metaphor with the example of the leap releases a tremendous, illustrative energy into the text. There is no denying that the effect of conventional punctuation (by comparison with the lively hyphens and generally indecorously run-on sentences of the notebook version) is slightly deadening. But the hypotyposis is surely greater this time in the published version, thanks to the metaphor.

If we quickly pass to the following pair of passages (we will return later to the above ones) on opposition versus contraries, further resonances are generated with the previous sets of passages:

> III (a) For {we are right & know what by Reason are might be inferred as} we have it in evidence as fact, that the most influencive Errors have ever been {Truths} partial Truths mistaken for the whole Truth, Truths divorced from their correspond{in}ent and supporting opposites, and converted into contrary Falsehoods by being reciprocally unbalanced and disintegrated/ {The writer Man may be an eloquent, learned, and acute Disputant; but he is not yet a Philosopher.} Many {there} are <the Learned> in every age who {deserve} may claim our admiration as {Men of Learning} eloquent Advocates, {acute Disputants,} or doughty Controversialists, indefatigable in research and subtle in discrimination, acute in the detection, and luminous in the exposure of fallacy and defect; but he alone deserves the name of a Philosopher, who has attained to see and learnt to supply the difference between Contraries that preclude, and Opposites that reciprocally suppose and require, each the other. (*CN* 3: 4326; { } denotes crossed out passages)

> (b) Permit me to draw your attention to the essential difference between opposite and contrary. Opposite powers are always of the same kind, and tend to union, either by equipoise or by a common product. Thus the + and − poles of the magnet, thus positive and negative electricity are opposites. Sweet and sour are opposites; sweet and bitter are contraries. The feminine character is opposed to the masculine; but the effeminate is its contrary. Even so in the present instance, the interest of permanence is opposed to that of progressiveness; but so far from being contrary interests, they, like the magnetic forces, suppose and require each other. (*C&S* 24n)

In Lecture 7 of 9 December 1811, Coleridge further wrote:

> (c) ... there is an effort in the mind when it would describe what it cannot satisfy itself with the description of, to reconcile opposites and to leave a middle state of mind more strictly appropriate to the imagination than any other when it is hovering between two images: as soon as it is fixed on one it becomes understanding and when it is wav(er)ing between them attaching itself to neither it is

imagination. (See Engell's and Bate's *BL* 1: 301–2n for this quotation)

In these passages, Coleridge seems to be arguing that the importance of the distinction made is quite simply incalculable, because it is exemplary of the distinction between imagination and fancy, of reason and understanding, implicitly described in the first two sets (I and II) of passages. The serpent's motion, the water insect's progress, like the imagination, moves by means of opposition. Metaphor is the representative par excellence of opposition; indeed it is often defined as the bringing of opposites or extreme differences into close contiguity with each other in order to produce a startling, but revealing relation. "Difference in similarity" is another way of describing metaphor, that "vehicle" of the imagination. Once again Coleridge resorts to metadiscourse ("Permit me to draw your attention"; "Even so in the present instance ...") in the published version. (Note also that the serpent metaphor quoted above (Ib) follows immediately on the *Church and State* passage (IIIb) as an "example" of it.) And, as in many original manuscripts, the crossing-out and lack of conventional punctuation, added to awkward syntax, tend to heighten the effect of hypotyposis. These passages are not without other subtleties, however, as we note the juxtaposition of three "examples" against the final serpent "metaphor" in the *Church and State* version (by putting together IIIa and Ib). Are "examples" of this kind contraries or opposites to "metaphors"? Coleridge imbeds another similar question in the notebook passage when he contrasts the "true philosopher" and the "men of learning": are they opposites or contraries? In the latter case, surely contraries, one could hazard, while in the former, opposites. Whatever we conclude, however, the interest is in his imbedding of the very issue discussed into his style, a quite incredibly sophisticated rhetorical device.

In this (all too brief) glance at passages (much subtle and detailed analysis of which must be left to the assured appreciation of our reader), the next set of passages adds yet more dimension to Coleridge's efforts to use classical rhetoric for the sake of characterising the nature of imaginative thinking:

IV (a) To return to the Question of Evil – woe to the man, to whom it is an uninteresting Question – tho' many a mind, overwearied by it, may shun it with Dread/ and here, N.B. scourge with deserved & lofty Scorn those Critics who laugh at the discussion of old Questions – God, Right & Wrong, Necessity & Arbitrement – Evil, &c – No! forsooth! – the Question must be new, new spicy hot Gingerbread, {from} a French Constitution ... change of Ministry ... – &c – Something new, something out of themselves – for whatever is in them, is deep within them, must be old as elementary Nature. To find no contradiction in the union of old &

novel – to contemplate the Ancient of Days with Feelings new as if they then sprang forth at his own Fiat – this marks the mind that feels the Riddle of the World, & may help to unravel it. But to return to the Question – the whole rests on the Sophism of imagining Change in the case of positive Substitution. (*CN* 1: 1622)

(b) My main objection is that this [i]s not the [t]rue history [o]f the Process and Progress of a mind that instinctively feels and would fain, solve the Riddle of the World and of itself –. (Fichte marginal comment)

(c) It was the union of deep feeling with profound thought; the fine balance of truth in observing, with the imaginative faculty in modifying the objects observed; and above all the original gift of spreading the tone, the *atmosphere*, and with it the depth and height of the ideal world around forms, incidents, and situations, of which, for the common view, custom had bedimmed all the lustre, had dried up the sparkle and the dew drops. "To find no contradiction in the union of old and new; to contemplate the ANCIENT of days and all his works with feeling as fresh, as if all had then sprung forth at the first creative fiat; characterizes the mind that feels the riddle of the world, and may help to unravel it ... this is the character and privilege of genius, and one of the marks which distinguish genius from talents ... its most unequivocal mode of manifestation ... genius produces the strongest impressions of novelty, while it rescues the most admitted truths from the impotence caused by the very circumstance of their universal admission. Truths ... are too often considered as *so* true, that they lose all the life and efficiency of truth, and lie bed-ridden in the dormitory of the soul, side by side with the most despised and exploded errors." (*BLS* 1: 59, quoted only approximately from *Friend*, see 2: 73–4)

(d) It is as trite as it is mournful, but yet most instructive and by the genius that can produce the strongest impressions of novelty by rescuing the stalest and most admitted Truths from the impotence caused by the very circumstance of their universal admission/ (admitted so instantly as never to be reflected on, never by that sole key of Reflection admitted into the {door} effective legislative Council-chamber of the Heart) so true that they lose all the privileges of Truth, and, as extremes meet, by being Truisms correspond in utter inefficiency with universally acknowledged Errors – (*CN* 2: 2535)

These passages illustrate the importance of the previous emphasis upon opposition as one of the primary modes of activity of the imagination, the opposition of old and new, of novel and familiar, truths that are "dead" truths, virtual errors. Here Coleridge attributes to Genius the ability to reconcile these opposites of new and old, familiar and novel, thought and feeling; indeed, the passages recall his anticipation of Keats's idea of negative capability in Lecture 7 quoted above (IIIc). In the notebook passage, it is suggested that failure of oppositional, imaginative thinking is the source of actual Evil. The craving after the new, "new spicy hot Gingerbread," uncounterbalanced by a craving for the ancient, leads to evil. The metaphor of the "riddle of the world" must have struck Coleridge as apt, since we find it in the notebooks, the marginalia, *Biographia*, and *The Friend*. In the two published versions and the final notebook entry, a further metaphor enriches the first one, of bed-ridden truths in the dormitory of the soul, while that passage is further strengthened by the contrast between genius and talent, a distinction already met in IIIa: namely, "Men of Learning" and the "true philosopher." Hypotyposis occurs in all three passages, most effectively perhaps in (a) and (c), as Coleridge achieves what he describes as the hallmark of genius through his metaphors: "the strongest impressions of novelty, [while rescuing] the most admitted truths from the impotence ..." etc.

Reminiscent of Shelley's insistence on "dead metaphor" (itself a living metaphor!) and the need to strip the veil of familiarity from the scene of things in order to revitalise dead metaphor, these passages invoke a strong sense of audience even in the private jottings, through varieties of metadiscourse, such as "To return to the Question of Evil," "But to return to the Question," "my main objection," – not to mention the conversational interjections which heighten the hypotyposis. This conversational tone is most consistent in the marginalia, where the reader has the most extraordinary sense of being in Coleridge's presence, hearing him speaking as if alive, partly because he himself seems to feel the corresponding vividness of the author's personality, and directs himself as if in speech to a living writer instead of a book. (Or to the owner of the book, who was sure to read his notes?)

Coleridge often turns to indirect and direct incantations to his reader about the best mode of reading, about the need to read in this imaginative, revitalising way. That is, he insists that if the author is to come alive for the reader, the reader must engage as genially and actively as possible. Hence, though in the above passages he pretends to speak only of the nature of Genius, his rhetorical import is directed as well at the reader who can see the analogy, rather than overlook the gems tossed out for indirect edification:

> V. Like a green field reflected in a calm and perfectly transparent lake, the image is distinguished from the reality only by its greater softness and lustre. Like the moisture or the polish on a pebble, genius neither distorts nor false-colours its objects; but on the contrary brings out many a vein and many a tint, which escapes the eye of common observation, thus raising to the rank of gems what

had been often kicked away by the hurrying foot of the traveller on the dusty high road of custom. (*BLS* 2: 121)

This passage is hypotyposis at its most intense; the gems "kicked away by the hurrying foot" of the reader are the metaphors and rhetorical strategies that go unnoticed when reading prosaically and hurriedly, both in the passage specifically, and throughout poetic prose writings. The move from a more passive to active simile, and then from simile to metaphor and hypotyposis, illustrates the indissoluble union of logic and rhetoric and is a well-calculated example of the narrative's serpent-like motion: "drawing up its voluminous train from behind on this fulcrum, [it] propels itself onward."

Numerous passages illustrate a much more direct appeal to the reader to engage imaginatively with texts in order to gain the most from them, whether it be the texts of Plato, Boehme, Wordsworth, Proclus, or Coleridge himself. As such, no special pleading is involved, since Coleridge argues that no text is experienced in depth without the reader's perception being the most imaginative kind possible. For example, he often returns to his maxim, "until you understand a writer's ignorance, presume yourself ignorant of his understanding" (see *BLS* 1: 160, *CN* 1: 928, and *CL* 3: 278). In this metadiscursive, rhetorical strategy, Coleridge seeks to enlist the reader's patience and geniality, by acknowledging the difficulty of the issues he presents and reassuring the reader thereby that what she finds difficult is genuinely difficult, and not her stupidity.

In a letter of September 1817, Coleridge explicitly argued, in a passage similar to one in Plato's *Symposium*:

> VI. it is the Intuition, the direct Beholding, the immediate Knowledge, which is the substance and true significance of all – But to give or to convey to another the Immediate is a contradiction in terms – all that a Teacher can do is, 1. to demonstrate the hollowness and falsehood of ... every ... scheme of Philosophy which commences with matter as a jam datum ... But the Truth of the Contrary must be seen – we must be it in order to know it. – 2. to excite the mind to the effort, and to encourage it by sympathy – (*CL* 4: 768, and see *BLS* 1: 167)

"To excite the mind to the effort" is the aim of Coleridge's lavish use of classical rhetorical skills, skills learnt more from Plato's *Dialogues* than anywhere else, arguably.

Two final sets of passages both discuss and, by hypotyposis, illustrate this role of the teacher and true philosopher:

> VII (a) The reader's Mind +heart+ Fancy are forced into too much action to sympathize with the merely Passive of our Nature – As little can the mind thus roused & awakened doze

+underthe+ and be brooded on by indistinct +Dreams & emfeebling Emotions+ Passions, as the low lazy Mist can creep upon the +Lake+ surface while a strong Gale is driving the Lake on in waves and billows before it – (*CN* 3: 4115)

(b) The reader is forced into too much action to sympathize with the merely passive of our Nature. As little can a mind thus roused and awakened be brooded on by mean and indistinct emotion, as the low, lazy mist can creep upon the surface of a lake, while a strong gale is driving it onward in waves and billows. (*BLS* 2: 16)

Earlier, in passage V, Coleridge had used the surface of the lake and the phenomenon of reflection as a metaphor for mind and thinking, that is, "reflection," but this metaphor suggests passivity only if taken literally. What is striking in the lake–mind metaphor is not the notion of passive reflection, but the emphasis on the purity and clarity of recreation. Only the familiarity of habit makes us forget how fascinating it is to watch natural surroundings beautifully recreated in the glassy surface of a lake. But this brings up another central issue, namely, that of the distinction between primary and secondary imagination, further discussed below.

Our final set of quotations is one of the most original of Coleridge's extended metaphors working in the service of hypotyposis:

VIII (a) And what is Faith? – it is to the spirit of Man the same Instinct, which impels the chrysalis of the horned fly to build its involucrum as long again as itself to make room for the Antennae, which are to come, tho' they never yet have been – O the Potential works in us even as the Present mood works on us! (*CN* 3: 4088)

(b) They and they only can acquire the philosophic imagination, the sacred power of self-intuition, who within themselves can interpret and understand the symbol, that the wings of the air-sylph are forming within the skin of the caterpillar; those only, who feel in their own spirits the same instinct, which impels the chrysalis of the horned fly to leave room in its involucrum for antennae yet to come. They know and feel, that the potential works in them, even as the actual works on them. (*BLS* 1: 167)

The question may be faith in the notebook entry, but by the *Biographia* version, it had become a metaphor in the service once again of characterising how truth is apprehended, how little a teacher can give in the way of dogma, but how much in the way of stimulating to effort. Metadiscourse and hypotyposis operate together: the covert and at times overt subject matter is the nature of imaginative activity and thinking, that "philosophic imagination" which Coleridge tries to help his reader to know by becoming herself imaginative. As author, he strives to encourage and provide those metaphoric hypotyposes which inspire to imaginative response, such as the image of the chrysalis. Such passages debunk, as do innumerable others, the notion that a writer centrally committed to notions of growth, activity, and potentiality (to process over product, to act over substance, and to imagination as the very basis of perception itself – not merely a trait of artistic activity) is correctly characterised as someone gazing in hypnotic trance on the timeless, unchanging perfection of reality. Like Shelley, Coleridge's writings paint a picture of an apocalyptic universe and the spiritual nature of the human being as in constant growth, change, and evolution, through the power of words and imaginative thinking.[6]

PERCEPTION AS IMAGINATION

Coleridge's rhetorical strategies create a poetic prose which seeks to reflect its subject matter in the style, by displaying a self-consciousness about the language used. An unusual, continuous attention, and at times energetic thinking, is demanded from the reader, as most rewarding texts must require. The idea of energetic thinking involves the concept of "passion," which Coleridge evoked in seeking to describe the specific nature of imaginative activity, that characteristic of the highest poetry. To arouse the reader to a corresponding "passion," to exhort the reader to exercise and strengthen her faculties of thought, Coleridge creates imaginative "encounters" between author and reader through metaphoric hypotyposis, usually involving meta-discursive implications. The drama of imaginative thinking, that philosophic imagination, is made so life-like as to happen to the reader herself. The "more continuous and equal attention" leads to "self-circling energies" of imaginative thinking and response. We are helped to grasp the difficult truth, that perception and analogous activities are (in a primary, essential way) imaginative, creative activities, not passive, receptive states.

That Coleridge's primary/secondary imagination distinction continues to be poorly understood is not really puzzling. The tyranny of custom, the veil of familiarity, the deadening results of habit (as I.A. Richards noted a half-century ago)[7] continue to blind us to the essentially creative, oppositional character of basic perception itself, of which artistic activity is a secondary echo. This (at first shocking) reversal of priorities is a very deconstructive gesture, as is Coleridge's second move, namely to reconcile the two apparent opposites of basic perception and artistic creation (after reversing their priorities), so that they become intimately related functions of each other, different in mode of operation, but not different in kind. Coleridge's distinction is closely involved in Platonic and neo-Platonic ideas about imitation (though he alters the terminology to speak more intelligibly to his early nineteenth-century audience). For the later writings of Plato, his lucubrations in the *Sophist* on "true imitation" (and in the *Timaeus*) lead to Shelleyan notions of the universe as a work of art, while Neoplatonists toy with further speculations that, very possibly, contain the germ of Coleridge's view of perception as primary and imaginative, and of the universe as correlative artifact.

KATHLEEN WHEELER

NOTES

1. On hypotyposis and the related concept, "enargeia," see also Plutarch, *Moralia* 346f–348d, who credits Thucydides with bringing narrative to life, as well as for vividness of style, and for rousing the reader's mind.
2. Bhavabhuti, Kalidasa, and Bhasa are some writers of note in this context. See especially "Shakuntala" and "Rama's Later History."
3. See, for example, the complicated framework of the *Symposium*, the *Theatetus*, and the *Parmenides*.
4. Jean Pierre Vernant, "Greek Tragedy: Problems of Interpretation," in *The Structuralist Controversy: The Language of Criticism and the Science of Man*, ed. Richard Macksey and Eugenio Donato (Baltimore: Johns Hopkins U.P., 1972), 273–89.
5. John Dewey, that is, who develops his criticism of the so-called "spectator theory of knowledge" in, for example, *Experience and Nature* (Chicago and London: Open Court Publishing Co., 1925).
6. See John W. Wright, *Shelley's Myth of Metaphor* (Athens, Georgia: University of Georgia P., 1970), for a lucid discussion of this issue.
7. I.A. Richards, *Coleridge on Imagination* (London: Kegan Paul & Co., 1934 [revised Bloomington, 1960]).

"The electric fluid of truth": The Ideology of the Commonwealthsman in Coleridge's The Plot Discovered

I

A modern-day William Pitt, feverishly hunting for imagined plots, might be tempted to think that there is among Coleridge scholars a plot to ignore the political pamphlet *The Plot Discovered*. The years leading up to the bicentennial of the French Revolution in 1989 saw the publication of a number of studies about the early political career of S.T. Coleridge, several of which attempted to contextualise the poetry and prose of this period of the poet's life.[1] *The Plot Discovered*, Coleridge's last substantial Bristol political publication, however, only figures marginally in their accounts of Coleridge's thought at this time. Generally it is used in the context of Coleridge's biography, illustrating his residence and activities in Bristol, and the beginnings of his friendship with the metropolitan radical John Thelwall. This is possibly for a number of reasons. Most prominently *The Plot Discovered* is a derivative work, largely dependent upon James Burgh's three volume encyclopaedia of Commonwealthsman ideology, *Political Disquisitions*, and contemporary debates and arguments about the recent measures of William Pitt's government. Lucyle Werkmeister, in the only sizeable treatment of the work which I know of, dismisses it as neither original nor good. The only question of any interest to her is, "why did Coleridge publish it at all?"[2] John Colmer in his pioneering work *Coleridge: Critic of Society* (1959) described the pamphlet as the work of "an excitable young man whose sensibilities had been outraged."[3] Colmer and Werkmeister substantially underrate Coleridge's political courage in publishing a work that could have been described as both treasonable and seditious. Both writers also fail to appreciate the highly allusive strategy of the pamphlet which appeals to a long tradition of radical thought, stretching back to the 1640s. In this essay I wish to suggest that *The Plot Discovered* is not only a very radical document but also an extremely rich one, and one which finds its best comparisons not among the radical pamphleteering of the 1790s, but with a despairing "jeremiad" such as Milton's *The Readie & Easie Way to Establish a Free Commonwealth* (1660).

Certainly the work, at first glance, appears less exciting (and less susceptible to anthologising) than its Bristol predecessor, *Conciones ad Populum* (1795), with which it has usually been compared. It eschews the more extreme elements of Coleridge's political radicalism in its concentration on constitutional issues and avoids the prophetic and millenarian tone that characterises much of the *Conciones ad Populum*.[4] In any case the work was published after the Two Bills which it criticised had become law, and lacks some of the improvisational immediacy which one gleans from the earlier political prose and poetry. As the notice in the *Annual Review* put it rather wistfully, "*Actum est!*"[5] Yet Coleridge's *The Plot Discovered* is not unique in being published after it was too late to be effective. That in itself should not disqualify a political tract from being taken seriously. It should also be remembered that both editions of Milton's *Readie & Easie Way* were written when the "Good Old Cause" was virtually moribund and when their author had little hope of changing anything.

The Plot Discovered is, however, an interesting work in many ways. First, it is in this work that Coleridge is closest to the concerns of the metropolitan radicals, though ironically this happens just at the time when the radical consensus established after the Treason Trials of 1794 begins to break up. It also marks the movement of Coleridge's political ideas from one phase to another, as he abandons the millenarian aspects of his thought and concentrates more clearly on the ideal of the Commonwealth.[6] It is with this tradition of thought that this essay is concerned. In it I would like to demonstrate the relationship of Coleridge's radical religious and political dissent to the ideology of republicanism which he encountered in many earlier writings, in particular, the prose tracts of Milton and James Burgh's Commonwealthsman encyclopaedia *Political Disquisitions* (1774–75). I should like to argue for a continuum of radical thought, a shared set of ideas and concepts which influence religious radicalism since the seventeenth century and which were held by Coleridge. I do not wish to argue for the direct influence of radical thinkers, as these ideas were explicated in several sources and, in some ways, have no common author, merely to claim that Coleridge, as a Unitarian dissenter, was heir to a tradition of a large body of radical thought, which he was able to draw upon as precedents for his own dissent.

II

The Plot Discovered should be seen against two backgrounds which are in no way mutually exclusive. It should be seen as a part of the radical agitation in opposition to Pitt's Two Bills, and against a tradition of radical religious and political dissent, which has it origins in the general leftward drift in theology occasioned by the Reformation. This is particularly so because both the government and the opposition, in the debate, were appealing to historical precedent in their arguments.

The Plot Discovered is published at a crucial time in the development of religious radicalism. The mid-1790s saw a splintering of the Reform movement between moderates and extremists and Christians and

Deists. As Marilyn Butler puts it, in this split the Unitarian Coleridge would find "his own intellectual position horribly compromised."[7] The Treason Trials of 1794 had failed in their immediate object to convict the leading reformers on a charge of High Treason, yet, in essence, the government plan had succeeded. The acquittal of John Thelwall, Thomas Hardy, and John Horne Tooke may have been received with enthusiasm in London and the provinces but the reform movement was soon to be in total disarray.[8] The repressive policies of the government effectively broke the reform movement (Goodwin, 362–3). As Nicholas Roe points out, "for Coleridge and Thelwall the winter of 1795–6 was to prove the last moment when a concerted effort for reform seemed practicable."[9] Carl B. Cone noticed that there was a definite change in the quality of radical agitation after the trials. The decline of the more moderate Society for Constitutional Information at this time marks an end of a phase of radical politics. This phase had originated with the Levellers of the English Revolution, surviving through the Restoration and flowering for the last time in the millenarianism of Joseph Priestley and Richard Price, and in Major John Cartwright's "vague and absurd" reading of English history.[10] This phase of thought also finds its expression in Coleridge's Bristol lectures, and, in a sad historical irony, it was being supplanted just as his radicalism reached its height. Soon pseudo-historical generalisations about Anglo-Saxon democracy and Commonwealth republican ideology would be replaced by emphatic avowals of deistic Paineite "rights of man philosophy," which were incompatible with Coleridge's scripturally based religious radicalism. In many ways, despite its derivativeness, or maybe because of it, Coleridge's *The Plot Discovered* is one of the last practical statements of the old Commonwealthsman ideal.

The immediate genesis of Coleridge's work was the series of events which succeeded John Thelwall's speech at the meeting organised by the London Corresponding Society at Copenhagen Fields on 26 October 1795 (Goodwin, 385). Thelwall warned the king that if "he ceased to consult the interests and happiness of the people, he will cease to be respected," adding that "Justice is a debt which a Nation hath a right to expect from the throne!" Thelwall rather unguardedly expressed his admiration for the revolution in France: "I venerate, I esteem, I adore the principles on which the French Revolution has been established."[11] Three days after Thelwall's utterance, the King's coach was mobbed on its way to the state opening of parliament by a group shouting "No Pitt" and "Bread." A window of the coach was shattered, probably by a stone, although George III believed himself to have been shot at. The mob was probably driven to protest by hunger and economic hardship but the government suspected that political agitators were at work (Goodwin, 386–7).[12] Their response was swift, introducing Two Bills to curtail the rights of assembly and petition. The first of the Two Bills, the Treasonable Practices Bill, was introduced by Grenville in the Lords on 6 November. It extended the scope of High

Treason, and resurrected the doctrine of "constructive treason" which Lord Chief Justice Eyre had unsuccessfully formulated in the Treason Trials of 1794. The second of this brace of measures was the Seditious Meetings Bill which restricted the right of meeting to 50 people, over which number permission had to be obtained from a magistrate. Furthermore this bill had a clause, specifically aimed at the political lectures of John Thelwall, classing all lecture rooms as "disorderly houses." Here was the Convention Bill that radicals had predicted and feared since 1794.[13] E. P. Thompson refers to the period stemming from the introduction of the Two Bills, or Gagging Acts as they became known, to the Royal assent received on 18 November as the "last, and greatest, period of popular agitation" of that century.[14] It is to this period of agitation that *The Plot Discovered* belongs.

Coleridge's response to the measures was to give a "Lecture on the Two Bills" on 26 November which was published in a much revised form as *The Plot Discovered* probably between 4 and 6 December.[15] The work draws heavily upon contemporary sources, specifically the speeches of Charles James Fox and the opposition within the Commons, the resolutions and addresses of the reforming societies, and Thelwall's lectures prior to the passage of the Bills. Coleridge's contemporary sources have been well-documented by Lewis Patton and Peter Mann in their edition of Coleridge's *Lectures 1795 On Politics and Religion (LPR)*. I would now like to move away from the context of Coleridge's contemporaries to that of the historical precedents for his arguments.

III

Coleridge's early religious and political dissent owed something to a tradition of radical thought which developed from the English Revolution in the 1640s. Coleridge planned to give a series of six lectures under the title "A Comparative View of the English Rebellion under Charles the First, and the French Revolution" in Bristol beginning on 23 June and continuing once a week (*LPR* 253–6). Although it is unlikely that these lectures were ever given, they show Coleridge's desire to ground his dissent on a more historical basis. The second lecture was to be concerned with:

> The Liberty of the Press. Literature – its revolutionary Powers. Comparison of the English with the French political Writers at the time of the several Revolutions. MILTON. SYDNEY. HARRINGTON. BRISSOT. SEYEYES. MIRABEAU. THOMAS PAYNE. (*LPR* 255)

During 1795–96, Coleridge filled the Gutch Memorandum Notebook with allusions and references to Toland's edition of Milton's prose works of 1678 and he was well aware of the writings of Commonwealthsmen like Harrington (*CN* 1: 39n, 106–10, 113–15, 118–19).[16]

For the Commonwealthsman, the model of the Rump Parliament which in 1649 abolished monarchy, and declared England to be "a Commonwealth and a Free State" became the ideal mode of government. The picture of the Rump as composed of serious revolutionaries gained credit over the century. Indeed there were ardent republicans within it, such as the regicides, Thomas Scot, Henry Marten, Thomas Chaloner, as well as the more famous Henry Neville, Algernon Sidney and Sir Henry Vane jr. Gradually this idea of the Rump's revolutionary republican nature gained currency. This assessment of the Rump has long been rejected by historians. Blair Worden persuasively argues that:

> The inauguration of the Commonwealth proved to be the end, not the beginning, of the Long Parliament's revolutionary measures, and the regime left in its wake a trail of disillusionment and resentment among the advocates of social and religious reform.[17]

Nevertheless to a substantial body of eighteenth-century reformers, desiring a sovereign, single-chamber parliament, the Rump became a yardstick with which to measure contemporary corruption. At first this idea of the Rump's revolutionary status grew in opposition to the Protectorate, as those discontented with, or alarmed by, Cromwell's personal rule, such as surviving Levellers and religious sectaries, combined in their disillusionment to idealise the dissolved parliament.[18]

The idealisation of the Rump Parliament continued, among reformers, throughout the eighteenth century in such works as James Burgh's *Political Disquisitions* and the anonymous *Historical Essays on the English Constitution* (1771). Such readings of the events of the 1640s and 1650s were generally based on a muddled and schematic view of what happened and bore little relation to the actual behaviour of the parliament itself. Nevertheless this republican myth was to provide a potent rallying call for all those dissatisfied with the ambition of ministers and their corrupt parliaments. Clearly it was a reading of history which was very influential in the 1790s. The formulaic invocation of the names of Milton, Sidney, and Harrington as patriots opposed to monarchical tyranny was common among the Friends of Freedom. In *The Plot Discovered* Coleridge himself somewhat ahistorically lumps together the "Sages and patriots that being dead do yet speak to us, spirits of Milton, Locke, Sidney, Harrington" (*LPR* 290). Wordsworth in 1802 made a similar appeal, but adding the name of Marvell:

> Great men have been among us; hands that penned
> And tongues that uttered wisdom – better none:
> The later Sidney, Marvel, Harrington,
> Young Vane, and others who called Milton friend.
>
> (*WPW* 3: 116)[19]

Neither Wordsworth nor Coleridge show any real understanding of the differences between these republican heroes. Milton and Harrington were not close political associates and substantially differed in their respective political programmes: Milton, eventually, favouring a permanent council of the godly as a government, whereas the Harringtonians argued for a rotating system of representation.[20] Such discriminations were, however, seldom made in the 1790s.

One of the main tenets of Commonwealthsman ideology which the eighteenth-century reformers appealed to was that of lost rights and the Norman Yoke of kingship. Milton had used the doctrine freely to attack the monarchy of Charles I. Coleridge and other radicals of the 1790s frequently looked back to pre-Conquest sources and seventeenth-century precedents which they combined with a religious egalitarianism learnt from scripture. The myth of the Norman Yoke of kingship is well described by Christopher Hill:

> Before 1066 the Anglo-Saxon inhabitants of this country lived as free and equal citizens, governing themselves through representative institutions. The Norman Conquest deprived them of this liberty, and established the tyranny of an alien King and landlords. But the people did not forget the rights they had lost. They fought continuously to recover them, with varying success. Concessions (Magna Carta for instance) were from time to time extorted from their rulers, and always the tradition of lost Anglo-Saxon freedom was a stimulus to ever more insistent demands upon the successors of the Norman usurpers.[21]

This myth also had a religious application which particularly appealed to the Unitarians. The Anglo-Saxon Church could be historically imagined as a primitive Church practising a Christianity uncorrupted by the ecclesiastical hierarchies which the Conquest introduced, subjecting England to the rule of the Pope (Hill, 60). Milton linked the Conquest with the rise of Antichrist in *Of Reformation* (*MPW* 1: 614).[22] Another version of the myth was Tacitus' formulation of the lost rights of ancient German liberties. Robert Southey's sixth historical lecture in Bristol discussed the "Manners and Irruptions of the Northern Nations" and Coleridge, who claimed partial authorship of Southey's lectures, printed part of it in the third number of *The Watchman*.[23]

The opponents of Charles I used the myth of the Norman Yoke against him. Its appeal was to give historical authenticity to radical demands. The Rump MP Thomas Scot could argue in defence of his regicide that "there was nothing but a House of Commons" in Saxon times.[24] Milton writes in *Of Reformation* how "our Progenitors that wrested their liberties out of the *Norman* gripe with their dearest blood and highest prowesse" (*MPW* 1: 592). In 1646 rank and file soldiers of the New Model Army could ask, "What were the Lords of England but William the Conquerour's Colonels? or the Barons but his Majors? or the Knights but his Captains?"[25]

Gerrard Winstanley also made frequent use of the idea. He argued that the death of Charles I marked the end of the Norman Yoke and its creation, propertied society. Winstanley and his Diggers justified their position to Fairfax and his Council of War in 1649:

> Seeing the common people of England by joynt consent of person and purse have caste out Charles our Norman oppressour, wee have by this victory recovered ourselves from under his Norman yoake, and the land is now to returne into the joynt hands of those who have conquered – that is, the commonours – and the land is to bee held noe longer from the use of them [the commoners] by the hand of anye [who] uphold the Norman and kingly power still.[26]

Winstanley's dismissal of property rights and his attempts to practice this by digging and cultivating the common land of St George's Hill, near Cobham in Surrey in 1649 strongly anticipates Coleridge and Southey's pantisocratic project which was based on a small familial community who were to engage in the cultivation of common property.[27] Winstanley used the theory of the Norman Yoke to attack the franchise itself, arguing that "the violent bitter people that are Freeholders" and able to vote are really "the *Norman* Common Souldiers, spread abroad in the Land." The members of parliament they elect are mandated "to Establish that Norman power the more forcibly over the enslaved *English*, and to beat them down again, when as they gather heart to seek for Liberty."[28]

Hill identifies three main interpretations of the Norman Conquest in the era of the Puritan Revolution which were used against royalist absolutism. First there was what became the Whig interpretation which argued that the common law was the embodiment of Anglo-Saxon liberties, stressing the sanctity of property. Secondly there existed the more radical version of the Levellers which suggested that the law itself legitimised inequality. The Levellers argued for a wider extension of the franchise to restore pre-Conquest equality. The most extreme version was that of Winstanley and the Diggers who advocated the end of private property in land and the renewal of the community of ownership (Hill, 87–9). Hill's schematisation is useful in assessing the degree of reform demanded by differing groups, but it is also necessary to accept the breadth of interpretation possible here, which allows individual thinkers to move from one interpretation to another while holding an overall consistency. Certainly Coleridge's radicalism sometimes appears closest to Winstanley's and sometimes to that of the Levellers. It is doubtful that Coleridge or any of his contemporaries had any real understanding of the fissured nature of Civil War radicalism, yet the ideas which were transmitted to him through his reading of Milton, Harrington, Burnet, Burgh and others were to provide historical substance for the radicalism of the Bristol Lectures.

The historical perspective is also somewhat complicated in the eighteenth century by the achievement in 1688–89 of some of the reformers' demands. Hill argues that the revival of Norman Yoke theory towards the latter half of the eighteenth century was used to sanction agitation for a more democratic representation and government. Certainly this cluster of political ideas persists until the 1790s. Both Hill and Goodwin identify the anonymous *Historical Essay on the English Constitution* (1771) as one of the "most comprehensive" documents of Norman Yoke theory on the radical side.[29] Its author wished to return to the purity of the idealised democratic Saxon constitution. Like so many of the reformers, his aim was not so much revolution as the restoration of rights lost by the Conquest. He believed that the Revolution of 1688 had begun this process of recovery, but that it had not gone far enough. The principles of 1688 he identified as: an elective crown, annual consultation by the King of a national deliberative council (the *witema gemot* of the Saxons), local popular assemblies, a popular militia, and a judicial system based on trial by jury. These institutions he believed to have been introduced into Britain around 450 AD by the Saxons and brought to perfection by King Alfred. Representative government had ceased with the Conquest and what recoveries had been made were, he argued, being lost through the Triennial Act of 1694, the Land Qualification Act of 1711, and the Septennial Act of 1716. The *Historical Essay*'s programme of reform called for the restoration of annual parliaments, the extension of the franchise, secret ballot, and the elimination of the rotten boroughs (Goodwin, 50–1).[30] The document's main contribution to Norman Yoke theory was its idealisation of the role of King Alfred, who became something of a radical hero. Coleridge's Bristol publisher, Joseph Cottle, for one, was motivated enough to write his epic about King Alfred in 1798. The treatise had a very wide circulation and was widely quoted by Major Cartwright in *Take Your Choice* (1776). Both the members of the Society for Constitutional Information and the London Corresponding Society used it (Hill, 96–7). John Thelwall in *The Rights of Nature* (1796) presented a strikingly polemical version of the doctrine which claims Harold as an elected king:

> William the Norman having collected together, by general proclamation, the nobles and assassins, the princes, and the freebooters of the continent, selected from them an army of 60,000 men; and having obtained the pope's blessing, and, of course enlisted heaven upon his side, invaded England, murdered the elected prince, the nobles, and the freeholders, and seizing upon the lands of all who resisted, divided them among his followers.[31]

Wordsworth also, as David V. Erdman has demonstrated, accepted a version of the myth "that an ancient British Commonwealth had been maintained despite invasions and bad kings."[32] Coleridge quoted the *Historical Essay*'s account of Charles II's tyranny in *The Plot Discovered*, although he appears to take the material direct from Burgh's *Political Disquisitions* (*LPR* 305). Coleridge was fully aware of the political uses to which the appeal to lost rights could be put, and in *The Plot Discovered* he outlines his opposition to Pitt's measures in a style highly allusive to a century and a half of radical thought.

IV

Two days before his lecture on the Two Bills Coleridge borrowed Burgh's three-volume work from the Bristol Library Society. He did not return it until 23 December.[33] The fragmentary lecture printed by Patton and Mann is almost entirely dependent on this work (*LPR* 258–76). What is remarkable about Burgh's work is that it should make such an immediate, yet transitory, impression. As Patton and Mann suggest this may be because Burgh was a compiler rather than an original thinker (*LPR* xlviii). The attraction of the *Political Disquisitions* for Coleridge lay in what Burgh was compiling; it was the soundness of his doctrine rather than the brilliance of his arguments that led Coleridge to use him. In particular Coleridge praises Burgh's work for "the multitude and pertinence" of the "historic facts collected" (*LPR* 302–3).

Burgh was an attractive figure to Coleridge's Unitarian circle. He was a dissenting schoolmaster who held Anti-Trinitarian views who became, arguably, the main exponent of Commonwealthsman ideology during the reign of George III. Burgh had been a friend of the prominent radical Dr Richard Price who had converted him to Anti-Trinitarianism. He joined the group known as the "Club of Honest Whigs" in 1760, which also included Price and Benjamin Franklin.[34] This group consisted of a large segment of the leading dissenting clergymen and schoolmasters of the metropolitan area who shared interests in science and Commonwealthsman political thinking. Generally they traced their ideas back to the Interregnum, propagating the doctrine of the right of resistance, religious toleration, the extension of the franchise, shorter parliaments and the exclusion of placemen. They supported popular libertarian movements and, later, were sympathetic to the cause of the American revolutionaries.[35]

Burgh wrote the *Political Disquisitions* as a kind of political encyclopaedia. His aim was to castigate the men in power, the "ambitious or avariticious [sic] grandees" who followed their own selfish interests while the constitution established in 1688–89 drew "nearer to its ruin and our country lay bleeding" (*BPD* 1: v, xii). In opposition to the ambitious men of his own day, Burgh places the examples of the Long and Rump Parliament. For him Charles I is the archetype of the "desperate Tyrant" and the struggle against him of "his brave and free parliament" is for Burgh

> one of the most striking instances in the history of the world of the glorious effects produced by the love of liberty and their country in the uninfluenced minds of a set of honest and courageous representatives. (*BPD* 2: 6–7, 9)

Nevertheless Burgh is critical of the dilatoriness of the Long Parliament and he objects to the length of its sitting, justifiable only by exceptionable circumstances. His ideal form of government is, instead, that of the Rump, the "*English* republic, which was demolished by the villainous *Cromwell*." This Burgh believes to be one of "the most unmixed that ever was known" and "a true government by representation." Although Burgh dislikes Charles I, it is Cromwell, "the mock-patron of liberty," who is the real villain of *Political Disquisitions* for his dismissal of the Rump (*BPD* 1: 9, 2: 376–9). In Burgh the myth of the representative nature of the Rump has been truly established as a yardstick by which to measure and criticise eighteenth-century government. Burgh is more interested in the polemical uses of the Rump than in the historical accuracy of his investigations.

Like the true Commonwealthsman he is, Burgh stands for annual parliaments and against corruption. He deplores the inequality in the representation of the cities. Although not a believer in universal suffrage, he argues that "everyman has what may be called property" and that is constituted by "a life, a personal liberty, a character, a right to his earnings, a right to a religious profession and worship according to his conscience" (*BPD* 1: 37).

Burgh is well aware of the notion of the Norman Yoke and makes frequent appeals to Anglo-Saxon times as precedents for the restoration of lost rights. "Parliaments," he claims, "were originally annual; and antiently all the people voted at elections." Burgh hypothesises that previous to the Normans, parliaments must have been annual:

> In the *Saxon* times it cannot well be supposed, that parliaments could be longer than annual, were it only for one reason, viz. That the members of their *witema gemot*, or parliaments, were Mayors, or officers, who held their office only one year, at the end of which they were obliged to divest themselves of all power, and to assemble the people for a new election. (*BPD* 1: 83–4)

Milton also provides a precedent for Burgh who confirms the high place the poet holds in Commonwealthsman thought. Milton had commented in *Eikonoklastes* (1649) that the bill of his own time for the shortening of parliaments to three years "was but the *third* part of one good step towards that which in times past was our annual right" (*BPD* 1: 84–5; *MPW* 3: 398).[36] Having referred to Saxon and Miltonic authority, Burgh completes the familiar Commonwealthsman pattern of allusion by praising Alfred for his frequent parliaments and invoking Harrington's labours in showing how in "well-conducted states" the error of "suffering power to remain too long in the same hands" was avoided. Burgh completes his pseudo-historical reconstruction of past liberty by claiming that the "people's right of annually electing deputies" had been enjoyed "longer than *Magna Charta*, without violation, till the time of *Charles I*" (*BPD* 1: 104, 112, 130).

Burgh justifies his political opinions by reference to a time of ancient liberty. He attacks the corruption of eighteenth-century parliaments by the systematic bribery which has developed since 1688: "The *Stuarts* intended to establish absolute power in the prince" but "our bribing courts intend to establish absolute power in a junto of grandees." By contrast Burgh refers to the practice of the Saxons. No one who reads the history of England "will say that our ancestors the *Saxons*, ever thought of inviting men to serve the public by great salaries or pensions" (*BPD* 1: 402; 2: 3, 118). Neither did governments require standing armies in ancient times. These, "in the *Saxon* times," were under the "absolute command of the dukes, or heretochs, who were elected by the people" (*BPD* 2: 345). A standing army represented a threat to the nation and it accounted for the ease by which Cromwell established his personal rule: "that what in Charles I was called abominable tyranny was acted anew" by Cromwell and "the liberty folks" who by military force excluded "almost 100 members from the house because they were not of his side." Cromwell could not have done this without his army (*BPD* 2: 377–8). Strangely Burgh confuses the purging of the Long Parliament in 1648, when Pride excluded about 140 MPs, with the dissolution of the Rump in 1653, and his survey of events leading to the dissolution is muddled.[37] Yet the gist of his complaint is clear. For Burgh, as for most radicals, the only safeguard for a Commonwealth was in the creation of a popular militia, in the manner of Alfred (*BPD* 2: 404).

Thus, in his reading of Burgh, Coleridge encountered the traditions of thought and the major ideas of Commonwealthsman philosophy. Many of these ideas would already be familiar to him through his reading of Milton, William Frend, Joseph Priestley, and Richard Price, yet Burgh's version, although historically inept, is much better documented and more thorough than that of other dissenters.

V

The very title of Coleridge's pamphlet betrays its groundings in Commonwealthsman ideology. The phrase "plot discovered" recalls Milton's great millenarian prayer from the *Animadversions* (1641):

> Thou hast discover'd the plots, and frustrated the hopes of all the wicked in the Land; and put to shame the persecutors of thy Church; thou hast made our false *Prophets* to be found a lie in the sight of all the people, and chac'd them with sudden confusion and amazement before the redoubled brightnesse of thy descending cloud that now covers thy Tabernacle. (*MPW* 1:705)[38]

The phrase also occurs in Bishop Burnet's *History of His Own Times* which Coleridge had borrowed on 20 April 1795, probably for his projected course of Historical Lectures.[39] Burnet uses the phrase "a plot is discovered" in a headnote, to describe the Rye House conspiracy of 1683 to assassinate Charles II and the Duke of York. Burnet does not take the plot seriously, but he describes how a kind of general outcry or public hysteria spread which made it dangerous not to accept publicly the existence of the plot. Among those executed for alleged complicity was Algernon Sidney, who had sat in the Rump Parliament and who is named in *The Plot Discovered* as a "Sage and patriot."[40] The Rye House plot constitutes a historical parallel for the supposed attack on George III, and Coleridge is using this to suggest the similarity between the actions of Charles II and George III, a comparison which he will later develop more explicitly.

Coleridge's rhetorical strategy in *The Plot Discovered* is to imply that plots and conspiracies exist only in the suspicious minds of ambitious ministers, and this is the real "plot" which he had discovered. One of Coleridge's techniques is to develop a highly allusive style, working through images that appeal to the radical consciousness of the 1790s. This strategy can be seen in the very first lines of the work. Coleridge quotes the one-eyed millenarian Leveller Richard Rumbold as an answer to the Bishop of Rochester, Samuel Horsley's notorious statement in the Lords on 11 November 1795, that "the Mass of the People have nothing to do with the laws but to obey them" (*LPR* 285,285n).[41] Rumbold, an extreme republican, had been implicated in the Rye House plot of 1683 to assassinate Charles II. He was involved in Argyll's abortive invasion of Scotland of 1685 for which he was executed. Coleridge knew of his activities from his reading of Burnet's *History of My Own Times*. According to Burnet, Rumbold, in 1683, compassed the assassination of Charles and his brother:

> One *Rumbold*, who had served in Cromwell's army, came twice among them; and while they were in that wicked discourse, which they expressed by the term lopping. He upon that told them, he had a farm near *Hodsden* in the way to *New-Market*: And there was a moat cast round his house, thro' which the King sometimes past in his way thither. He said, once the coach went thro' quite alone, without any of the guards about it; and that, if he had laid anything cross the way to have stopt the coach but a minute, he could have shot them both ... Upon which they ran into much wicked talk about the way of executing that. But nothing was ever fixed on: All was but talk.[42]

The parallel with the supposed attempt on George III's life is clear. A plot is discovered, which is really not a plot, which imagines the shooting of the present king, travelling in his coach (although George III's business was more dignified than Charles II's), and this alleged conspiracy is used to further limit and restrain opposition to the government. Rumbold admitted to having been a guard at Charles I's execution, although his accusers claimed he was one of Charles's masked executioners. Burnet tells how Rumbold, fatally wounded by his captors, delivered a defiant speech before his somewhat redundant execution. It is from this that Coleridge quotes. He draws on both Burnet and Burgh for his recapitulation of Rumbold's words:

> We have entrusted to Parliament the guardianship of our liberties, not the power of surrendering them. Shame fall on the mitred mufti [i.e. Horsley], who aims to persuade us, that it is the Almighty's will that the greatest part of mankind should come into the world with saddles on their backs and bridles in their mouths, and the remaining few ready booted and spurred for the purpose of riding them. (*LPR* 285)[43]

Rumbold's striking metaphor of the riding of horses for political oppression was probably derived from standard Leveller rhetoric, in particular from John Lilburne's *An Anatomy of the Lords Tyranny* (1646) where the Leveller appeals against his incarceration for his criticism of the Earl of Manchester:

> if you were in jeast, when you did all this, and never intended, what you declared, but meerly set us a fighting to unhorse and dismount our old Riders & Tyrants, that so you might get up and ride us in their steads.[44]

Coleridge's audience would be expected to recognise the pedigree of this image in radical republican thought. Coleridge, however, does not mention Rumbold's name. This is surprising as Burgh directly quotes Rumbold, and Burnet is explicitly relating the events surrounding the rebel's execution. Coleridge's refusal to indicate Rumbold as a source, although his words would be familiar to many, is best understood as a signifying silence. He may well have decided that he had gone far enough in simply alluding to the speech at all, given the fact that Rumbold was executed for treason and, at the least, had been one of the guards at the scaffold of Charles I. To name Rumbold as a source, just as the government were in the process of substantially extending the present definition of treason, would have been extremely dangerous. As it was, Coleridge displayed great daring in using the words of such a notorious republican at all.

Coleridge's overall strategy in *The Plot Discovered* is to reveal the true motivation behind the introduction of Pitt's Two Bills and then to ground his resistance to the government in the context of the Commonwealthsman struggle against monarchical and ministerial tyranny. He argues that the real motive for proposing the new "Treasonable Practices Bill" is that the "existing laws of Treason were too clear, too unequivocal" for Justices to fool "English juries" with their elaborate legal formulations. Under the provisions of the new bill, Coleridge argues, anyone speculating that a Republic is "the most perfect form of government" would be guilty of High Treason (*LPR* 288–9). Likewise the real plots informing the second of the Two Bills, the "Seditious Meetings Bill," are "first that the people of England should possess no unrestrained right of consulting in common on common grievance" and "secondly ... Mr. Thelwall should no longer give political lectures." Coleridge refers here to the political lectures of John Thelwall, probably the leading reformer of his time, whose activities had so irritated the government. For Coleridge, Thelwall is not an "unsupported malcontent" but a spokesman for the many:

> But William Pitt knows, that Thelwall is the voice of tens of thousands, and he levels his parliamentary thunder-bolts against him with the same emotion with which Caligula wished to see the whole Roman state brought together in *one* neck, that he might have the luxury of beheading it at *one* moment. (LPR 296–7)[45]

The Two Bills are, for Coleridge, nothing more than an attempt to overthrow the settlement of 1688–89. Although in *Conciones ad Populum* Coleridge envisaged reform far beyond the Williamite consensus of 1688, in *The Plot Discovered* he is more closely, but not exclusively, concerned with constitutional issues, and the grounding of his argument in precedents. Yet, as we shall see, this in no way mitigates his desire for a dynamic and progressive constitution. Following Burgh, he argues that with the Bill of Rights of 1689, the constitution is sacrosanct: "now we cannot be *legally* undone even by a Parliament: for (as Bolingbroke remarks) Parliament cannot annul the Constitution" (*LPR* 301). If the constitution is violated then the people will have the right of resistance. It was one thing for Burgh to argue for the right of resistance in his weighty tomes of the 1770s, but to argue for it in the wake of the Treason Trials of 1794 in a political pamphlet was a very risky thing to do, and guaranteed to bring Coleridge to the attention of the government.

Lord Grenville when he introduced the Treasonable Practices Bill in the Lords on 6 November boasted of the precedents he had found for the bill in the "measures of our ancestors," assuring the House that the bill was "in a great measure copied from the act in the reign of queen Elizabeth, and the act of Charles 2nd, passed soon after the commencement of his reign."[46] Grenville's appeal to precedent dictates Coleridge's strategy as he investigates these precedents further. Appropriating the courtly tone of his lordship, Coleridge points out that the acts of Elizabeth were copied by James I and "deemed safe precedents by the first Charles," adding that such measures "good Lord Grenville, produced that civil commotion, *vulgarly* called, the great REBELLION!" Precedents can cut both ways. Coleridge, significantly, cites as his authority the influential *Historical Essay on the English Constitution* which Hill and Goodwin regard as so important in transmitting the myth of the Norman Yoke to the eighteenth century (*LPR* 303–5; Goodwin, 50–1; Hill, 95–6). The *Historical Essay* recounts the loss of the people's rights at the time of the Conquest and explains how the reigns of Charles II and George III were remarkably similar:

> Judgement and justice were directed by court-policy: severity and cruelty tooke the place of mercy and moderation: slitting of noses, cutting of ears, whipping, *pillorying*, branding, fining, *imprisoning, hanging*, and *beheading*, were the *constant lot of those who had virtue enough to speak, write or act in defiance of constitutional Liberty ... the House of Commons ... passed a Law, by which no man durst ask his neighbour to join him in a petition for relief to the King or either House of Parliament*. (Coleridge's italics; *LPR* 305)[47]

Coleridge attempts to expose Grenville's constitutional gloss as little more than an attempt to disguise tyranny. The Two Bills fall into a familiar historical pattern, easily identified by the Commonwealthsman, of monarchical tyranny and ministerial ambition. Grenville's appeal to the precedents of Elizabeth I and Charles II allows Coleridge to counter-appeal to the revolutions of 1649 and 1688 as the historical sequels to these precedents. Yet Coleridge does not wish for the simple restoration of the settlement of 1688–89. Behind his criticism of the Two Bills is a view of government which is dynamic and progressive.

VI

Coleridge was too systematic a thinker simply to attack the Two Bills on their own terms. In the *Conciones ad Populum* he had stressed the "necessity of *bottoming* on fixed Principles" (*LPR* 33), and in *The Plot Discovered* he characteristically attempts to place his remarks within a theoretical framework. The Two Bills sought to legislate against any attempt to excite hatred of the constitution. For this to be just, Coleridge argues that it must be proven that the British constitution had no imperfections that could cause dislike or hatred. Coleridge attempts a threefold categorisation of the forms of government in order to evaluate the alleged perfections of the British system:

> Governments have assumed many different forms; but in their essence and properties, all possible modes of Government are reducible to these three: Government *by* the people, Government *over* the people, and Government *with* the people. (*LPR* 306)

Coleridge argues that the first mode of government is only possible when "the affairs of the whole are directed by all actually present." This applies to the practice of ancient Athens and of some of the American tribes. It was also the proposed mode of Coleridge and Southey's pantisocratic venture. Clearly Coleridge believes this to be the ideal form of government. Of course this kind of political organisation could not be possible for a complex society. Coleridge thus allows that in cases such as these all may be "*morally* present, that is, where every man is represented, and the representatives act according to instructions." This he hopes will be the final state of the French government. Again we should not be misled by Coleridge's constitutional language into overlooking the fact that this is a very radical stance to take, especially during the period of Pitt's "British Terror." Although Coleridge does not name this kind of government, it is that of a democracy (although defined in patriarchal terms). The question as to whether or not this ideal form of representative democracy has any room for a monarch is not explored, but neither Athens, the American tribes, nor the French Republic had a king as defined in the British constitution. The antitype of this ideal is that of despotism, "in which the people at large have no voice in the legislature, and possess no other safe or established mode of political interference." This applies classically to the absolutisms of Spain and Turkey. The third form of government, which is supposed to be possessed by Britain, is that of "Government *with* the people." Governments of this kind are not meant to be static but should be moving towards the representative democracy envisaged in the first mode (*LPR* 306–7). Coleridge argues that the British constitution is one where the people have very little say in their choice of representatives:

> in the House of Commons three hundred and six are nominated or caused to be returned by one hundred and sixty Peers and Commoners with the Treasury, and three hundred and six are more than a majority: the majority therefore of the House of Commons are the choice, and of course the proxies of the Treasury.

The people thus exercise "no sovereignty either personally, or by representation" (*LPR* 308–9).

The only things that could distinguish the British government from a despotism, in Coleridge's eyes, were the liberty of the press and the right of petitioning, which he believed gave to the people an "*influential* sovereignty." The right of petitioning means that if "corruption deafen power" the voice of the people will be heard, expressed in tones "gradually increasing till they swell into a deep and awful thunder, the VOICE OF GOD" (*LPR* 312). The equation of the voice of the people with the voice of God was a central tenet of Milton's early political creed. In his *Defence of the People of England* (1651), he answered Salmasius' charge that, as Charles was appointed by God, only God could dethrone him, with the ringing assertion that:

> It is God who, wherever his infinite wisdom wills it, is wont to overthrow haughty and unruly kings who exalt themselves above the measure of mankind ... It was by his evident will that we were unexpectedly encouraged to hope for that security and liberty which had been well-nigh lost to us: We followed him as our leader ... we entered on a path ... revealed by his guidance.
> (*MPW* 4.1: 305)

Coleridge makes a direct allusion to Milton when he invokes his views on the petition, which is, as "Milton says, good old english for *requiring*" (*LPR* 313). Coleridge's reference is to *Eikonoklastes*, where Milton argued that petitioning "in better English, is no more than recquesting or requiring, and men require not favours onely, but thir due" (*MPW* 3: 461). The same passage is also quoted by Burgh (*BPD* 3: 438–9).[48] Significantly Coleridge's desire to cite Milton's authority leads him either to misunderstand or deliberately obfuscate the elder writer's point. In *Eikonoklastes* Milton's argument was a linguistic one, whereby he demystifies the latinate word "petition," favouring instead the English words "request" or "require." Coleridge rather misses this point in describing the word "petition" as "good old english" when it is clearly not an English word at all. But the presence of Milton is the main thing. He had also famously argued for the liberty of the press in *Areopagitica* which Coleridge, of course, knew well. There Milton describes the liberty of the press as "the peoples birthright and priviledge in time of Parlament" (*MPW* 2: 541). Coleridge's belief in the importance of the freedom of the press remained with him throughout his life. In his Essay "The Liberty of the Press" for *The Friend* (1809–10) he praises "the purifying effects of a free Press" which Britain has had "since the revolution." Coleridge opens this essay with a substantial extract from Milton's *Areopagitica* and cites again "our prophetic Harrington." Of course in 1809 Coleridge was keen to stress that the freedom of the press could be abused "in seditious and incendiary publications," and he allows the state to decide what constitutes such a publication (*Friend* 1: 70–6).

Coleridge fears that when the Two Bills become law Britain will actually be a despotism. No longer will men be able to consult in common on common grievances and the liberty of the press will be at an end. In this state no improvement would be possible as the bills were aimed at "all men who recommend reform" by pointing out the defects of the government. Coleridge describes how this lack of freedom will lead to stagnation and despair. Significantly, to express the state of Britain under Pitt's repression he uses an image from natural philosophy:

> By the operation of Lord Grenville's Bill, the Press is made useless. Every town is insulated: the vast conductors are destroyed by which the electric fluid of truth was conveyed from man to man, and nation to nation. (*LPR* 313)

The Bills act as insulation preventing the free dissemination of the truth. Coleridge here draws on the recent work on electricity of Franklin and Priestley, who postulated the fluidity of the phenomenon. Without the natural dissemination of truth acting upon the forces of inequality in society no progress is possible in the moral or social order. By placing the political in the realms of natural philosophy, Coleridge is implying that the spread of knowledge and liberty is a natural process.

Of course this process can be impeded by despotic insulation. Yet all this will mean in the longer term, following the logic of Coleridge's trope, is that the discharge will be more powerful and more violent. This explains the violence of the French Revolution and prophesies a similar storm if the lightning of reform is not allowed to discharge itself naturally, or aided by a sage and philosopher such as Franklin, who in Coleridge's millenarian poem "Religious Musings" (*PW* 1: 118; lines 234–59) tames the violence of the storm. It is also apparent that when the lightning does strike, as it inevitably must, it will hit the tallest structure in the land, i.e. the monarch. Behind Coleridge's equation of truth and electricity lies a grim warning to the establishment to reform if it wishes to avoid the storm of revolution.[49]

VII

Coleridge's *The Plot Discovered* constitutes a devastating attack on the motivations and competence of Pitt's government. It shows a mastery of the detail of constitutional precedent, and is an incisive and forensic examination of the nature and likely consequence of the Two Bills becoming law. John Thelwall, who had not yet encountered Coleridge personally, was motivated by the strength of its analysis to mention the pamphlet in the same sentence as the protest of the more celebrated political philosopher William Godwin:

> *Hume* might have been hanged for his "Idea of a Free Commonwealth", as Godwin has shewn in his "Considerations" – The future vendors of that work may be hanged, drawn and quartered, as Coleridge has shewn in his "Protest."[50]

Previous writing on *The Plot Discovered* has underestimated the radicalism of the pamphlet. Coleridge is arguing for a government that is in the process of becoming a democracy and he assesses the value of that government in terms of its proximity to, or distance from, that ideal. Neither is *The Plot Discovered* harsh and dry in its technique. Coleridge adopts a variety of stylistic strategies to express more forcefully his opinions. He shows great skill in the art of political caricature in the several jibes at Pitt and his ministers. Homing in on Pitt's verbal prolixity, Coleridge identifies this as a sign of the minister's moral duplicity. Pitt's "meaning generally bears an inverse proportion to the multitude of his words ... His style is infinitely porous ... the universe of his bills and speeches would take up less room than a nutshell" (*LPR* 296). The personal follies and inconsistencies of Pitt, Grenville, Dundas, and Windham are humorously exposed with almost Scriblerian wit (*LPR* 294, 296, 298, 302–3).[51] Coleridge's image of "British Liberty" after the passage of the bills has the bold lines and immediacy of a Gillray cartoon: she "leaves her cell by permission, and walks abroad to take the air between two jailors; fettered, and handcuffed, and with a gagg in her mouth" (*LPR* 314).

The Plot Discovered, however, is not an optimistic work. It closes with a version of the stock cautionary tale of the Danish people's surrendering of their rights to the King of Denmark. Coleridge anglicises the tale and presents it, ironically after what has previously been argued, in the form of a petition from the people of Denmark to their King, satirising the British public's willingness to allow Pitt to remove their liberties. It is this part of the pamphlet which provides the answer to Werkmeister's question, "Why does he publish it at all?" The notion that political freedom depends on virtue was, of course, a key Miltonic idea. In *The Readie & Easie Way* (1660) Milton had warned how "God in much displeasure gave a king to the *Israelites*, and imputed it a sin to them that they sought one." Like the prophet Samuel, Milton had warned them that *"ye shall cry out in that day because of your king whom ye shall have chosen, and the Lord will not hear you in that day"* (*MPW* 7: 424, 450). Coleridge's tone in *The Plot Discovered* recalls that of Milton's despairing Commonwealthsman tract. In his pamphlet Coleridge frequently adopts the Miltonic prophetic mantle. He envisages Pitt's Britain after the passage of the Two Bills in an apocalyptic context:

> All political controversy is at an end. Those sudden breezes and noisy gusts, which purified the atmosphere they disturbed, are hushed to deathlike silence. The cadaverous tranquility of despotism will succeed the generous order and graceful indiscretions of freedom – the black moveless pestilential vapour of slavery will be inhaled at every pore. But, beware, O ye rulers of the earth! For it was ordained at the foundation of the world by the King of kings, that all corruption should conceal within its bosom that which will purify; and THEY WHO SOW PESTILENCE MUST REAP WHIRLWINDS. (*LPR* 289)

The prophecies of Hosea, the natural philosphy of Erasmus Darwin, the millenarianism of Milton and Priestley are synthesised into a chilling image of political and social corruption. In its power and tone the vision recalls Blake's picture of London from *Songs of Experience* where the city is pictured in the grip of mental and social paralysis.

John Colmer claims that Coleridge is here parodying Burke's style.[52] Colmer, however, fails to realise that there is a long tradition in Protestant polemicising of this kind of political writing: that of the "jeremiad." James Holstun has shown how Milton's *Readie & Easie Way* can be classified as an "anti-utopian jeremiad," and Laura Lunger Knoppers, in responding to the apparent futility of Milton's publishing his work despite the certainty of the Restoration, finds an explanation for this in Holstun's categorisation. Here is her account of the jeremiad:

> The jeremiad is a prophetic lament over the decline of a covenant nation. The speaker of the jeremiad assumes the authority and

stance of the Old Testament prophets, looking to past ideal, present sin, and future judgement or blessing. The speaker depicts his nation by analogy, allusion, or metaphor as the New Israel, calling the nation to repent for violation of its covenant with God.[53]

Knoppers shows how the genre of the jeremiad can be applied to the polemical literature of the Civil War where Republican writers use the language of the jeremiad to interpret various political crises, bringing to bear typological categories to persuade their audience to repentance. This model of interpretation, as far as I know, has not yet been applied to the writings of religious radicals after the Civil War. It seems a very useful one to apply not only to *The Plot Discovered* but also to Coleridge's *Conciones ad Populum* and "Religious Musings." *The Plot Discovered* bears many of the stylistic features of the jeremiad, in particular its use of the alienated prophet Hosea who, along with Ezekiel and Jeremiah, is much favoured by writers in this genre. The closing pages of *The Plot Discovered* present a prophetic lament over the backsliding of the covenanted nation, looking back to a mythic past of "Sages and patriots" who are dead but "do yet speak to us" (*LPR* 290). Coleridge also, adopting the stance of the prophet, speaks to his nation by way of the analogies of "electric fluids" and "black pestilential vapours" and his closing political allegory. Significantly many of the writers of jeremiads on the Good Old Cause in 1659 identify themselves as Ezekiel's "watchmen,"[54] this being Coleridge's identification of himself in his political journal *The Watchman* (1796). The jeremiad speakers see themselves as acting out of a duty to God as much as from the hope that people will actually listen to what they say, and herein lies the answer to Werkmeister's question. In *The Plot Discovered* Coleridge, just as Milton and the beleaguered republicans of 1659–60, is acting as a witness against the apostacy of the British people. The actual passage of the Two Bills does not alter this. Through his adoption of the prophetic role in *The Plot Discovered* Coleridge defines his purpose, audience, and voice in terms of the prophet Hosea expecting the "curse of Heaven upon the nation" (*LPR* 316). Milton's *Readie & Easie Way* castigated the English people for desiring the return of the king, ascribing their motivation to the commonly held belief that "nothing but kingship can restore trade" and bring "more plentie and prosperitie" (*MPW* 7: 461–2). So Coleridge in his ironic petition savagely mocks those who expect peace and prosperity from kings:

> Henceforward we expect, that the treasures which are yearly scrambled for by the sons of clamour, will either remain with the people and increase their domestic comforts, or be drawn out for the reward of genius and virtue, and the promotion of arts, sciences, and true religion. Countless millions will no longer be expended to shed blood and bring famine and pestilence. (*LPR* 317–18)

Coleridge, as Milton before him, is making it plain that if the British people do not fight for their liberties then they will call down the "curse of Heaven" upon themselves. The tone is one of lament and prayer rather than of hope that the people will cease to backslide. Both prophets are, in a sense, bidding a last farewell to liberty: "Ere yet this foul treason against the majesty of man, ere yet this blasphemy against the goodness of God be registered among our statutes, I enter my protest!" (*LPR* 285). So Milton had called the concluding lines of his pamphlet perhaps "the last words of our expiring libertie" (*MPW* 7: 463). The only possible hope for either lies in the jeremiadic notion of the saving remnant (*MPW* 7: 363, 463); the pessimistic Coleridge promises to "join the still small voice of reason, ere yet it be overwhelmed in the great and strong wind, in the earthquake and in the fire!" (*LPR* 286). Both Coleridge and Milton appropriate a prophetic role; both act as witnesses even if it is too late for them to be heard. In the last paragraph of *The Readie and Easie Way* Milton quotes Jeremiah, saying "thus much I should perhaps have said though I were sure I should have spoken only to trees and stones; and had none to cry to, but with the Prophet, 'O *earth, earth, earth*! to tell the very soil itself what her perverse inhabitants are deaf to'" (*MPW* 7: 462–3). What James Holstun writes about Milton's pamphlet seems equally applicable to Coleridge's: "Milton's anti-utopian jeremiad opposes the virtuous reason of a lone prophet to the monstrous irrationality of the multitude."[55] The figure of the lone prophet who removes himself from political activity, denouncing the social collective, prophesying the downfall of his guilty nation, and willing to submit himself to whatever punishments history deems fit was a role which Milton adopted at the Restoration. This was, arguably, the role which Coleridge was to attempt to appropriate during the remainder of his life.

VIII

The Plot Discovered looks back to Coleridge's optimistic pantisocratic phase, as well as forwards to his later conservatism. The disillusionment with the British people seen at the close of the pamphlet presages Coleridge's abandonment of democratic values publicly represented in his poem "Fears in Solitude" (1798) where he criticises those who expect constitutional change to lead to moral improvement:

      Some, belike,
Groaning with restless enmity, expect
All change from change of constituted power;
As if a government had been a robe,
On which our vice and wretchedness were tagged
Like fancy-points and fringes, with the robe
Pulled off at pleasure.
    (*PW* 1: 261–2)

In so doing Coleridge is using the Commonwealthsman tradition to move from his radical reading of the constitution to one where the rights of property were sacrosanct. This shift, more than any other revision, marks the end of his radical phase. He publicly signalled this in his Essay for the *Morning Post* of 7 December 1799 "On the French Constitution." The pantisocratic view of property is completely abandoned:

> For the present race of men Governments must be founded on property; that *Government is good in which property is secure and circulates; that Government the best, which, in the exactest ratio, makes each man's power proportionate to his property*. (*EOT* 1: 32)

In *The Plot Discovered* Coleridge had declared that government to be best "where every man is represented, and the representatives act according to instructions" (*LPR* 306). By 1799 Coleridge is arguing that the basis of government should no longer be upon personal representation but upon property: the shift is crucial. No longer is the discharge of the "electric fluid of truth" a political necessity. Coleridge in 1799 is more interested in ways of insulating society from the too immediate enlightenment.

Shortly after his return from Germany, Coleridge gave a College Commemoration Sermon in October 1799, which survives in manuscript form. In it Coleridge strikes a Burkeian posture, arguing for the cherishing "of that sacred feeling of reverence for antiquity." He once more equates the realms of the natural and the political, reformulating his electric trope. Praising the wisdom of ancestors he tells how

> [our forefathers] never dreamt that whole People could be illuminated at once and by a convulsion as needles during a storm have been magnetized by a flash of Lightning ... They provided that *knowledge should be fundamentally & Gradually instilled*.[56]

Now institutions such as government and property become forms of insulation against the discharge of "the electric fluid of truth" which in its natural nakedness is too pure and severe for unfiltered dissemination. This passage anticipates Coleridge's idea of the clerisy in his later *On the Constitution of Church and State* (1829). In his essay "Government and Reason" from *The Friend* of 1809, Coleridge again uses the image of electricity to describe a political process, but once more it is a revisionary one. He argues that the inability of humanity to learn from experience leads it to extremes in politics:

> The horror of the Peasant's War in Germany, and the direful effects of the Anabaptist tenets, which were only nominally different from those of Jacobinism by the substitution of religious for philosophical jargon, struck all Europe for a time with affright. Yet little more than a century was sufficient to obliterate

> all effective memory of those events: the same principles budded forth anew and produced the same fruits from the imprisonment of Charles the First to the restoration of his Son ... and the same principles aided by circumstances and dressed out in the ostentatious garb of a fashionable philosophy, once more rose triumphant and effected the French Revolution.

Coleridge, as in his radical days, envisages the Puritan and French Revolutions as resulting from similar principles, expressed in different "jargon," but now both are seen as the results of fanaticism and not reason. Coleridge adapts his image of the lightning to describe the people's feelings of indignation and disgust which gradually charge up as does the storm cloud. Coleridge argues that memories of the "democratic phrenzy" of the Revolution are dim and that the crimes of Napoleon's despotism

> by little and little have drawn off to other objects the electric force of the feelings, which had massed and upheld those recollections; and that a favourable concurrence of occasions is alone wanting to awaken the thunder and precipitate the lightening from the opposite quarter of the political Heaven. (*Friend* 1: 179–80)

Now the storm is no longer identified with the natural progress of truth, whether gradual or violent. It corresponds instead to a kind of retaliatory polarity divorced from truth and motivated by spurious reasoning. Electricity may gather itself into a charge but lightning is arbitrary.

In 1795, however, neither the heavens nor the lightning were arbitrary and the "electric fluid" and truth were the same thing. *The Plot Discovered*, unlike *The Friend*, belongs to the great tradition of Commonwealthsman pamphleteering. In it we can see Coleridge's movement from virtual Diggerism, to Levellerism, with a trajectory towards his later conservative views of property. It is a concise and evocative pamphlet, fully characteristic of Coleridge's radical religious proselytising. Certainly it is not his greatest work, but neither is it as derivative and as dull as previous criticism has suggested. *The Plot Discovered* also demonstrates the depth of Coleridge's knowledge of seventeenth- and eighteenth-century political writing, arguing that while it is important to restore to Coleridge his lost contemporaries it is also crucial that we do not forget political ideologies older than those of William Godwin and Thomas Paine. If Coleridge's pamphlet recalls the work of any other radical polemicist, it must surely be the writings of that other great poet and republican John Milton.

PETER J. KITSON

NOTES

1. Nicholas Roe, *Wordsworth and Coleridge: the Radical Years* (Oxford: Clarendon P., 1988); idem., "Coleridge and John Thelwall: The Road to Nether Stowey," in *The Coleridge Connection*, ed. R. Gravil and M. Lefebure (London: Macmillan, 1990): 60–80; I. M. Wylie, *Young Coleridge and the Philosophers of Nature* (Oxford: Clarendon P., 1989); Robert Sayre, "The Young Coleridge: Romantic Utopianism and The French Revolution," *Studies in Romanticism* 28 (1989): 397–415; Peter J. Kitson, "Coleridge, the French Revolution, and 'The Ancient Mariner': Collective Guilt and Individual Salvation" and, David Jasper, "Preserving Freedom and Her Friends: A Reading of Coleridge's *Watchman (1796)*," in *The Yearbook of English Studies* 19 (1989): 197–207, 208–18.
2. Lucyle Werkmeister, "Coleridge's *The Plot Discovered*: Some Facts and A Speculation," *Modern Philology* 61 (1958–59): 254–63. Werkmeister argues that Coleridge deliberately falsified the date of the pamphlet's publication to avoid prosecution when the Two Bills became law on 18 December 1795. Werkmeister's speculations have been disproved by an earlier dating of the work. See Peter J. Kitson, "Coleridge's *The Plot Discovered*: A New Date," *NQ* 31 (1984): 57–8.
3. John Colmer, *Coleridge: Critic of Society* (Oxford: Clarendon P., 1959): 19–22.
4. For Coleridge's millenarianism see Wylie, *Young Coleridge*, 62–80, 113–21; H.W. Piper, *The Active Universe: Pantheism and the Concept of Imagination in the English Romantic Poets* (London: Athlone P., 1962): 47–59, 93–7; idem., *The Singing of Mount Abora: Coleridge's Use of Biblical Imagery and Natural Symbolism in Poetry and Philosophy* (London; Associated University Presses, 1987); idem., "Coleridge and the Unitarian Consensus," in *Coleridge Connection*, 273–90 (280–1); Peter J. Kitson, "Coleridge, Milton and the Millennium," *TWC* 17 (1987): 61–6; Tim Fulford, "Coleridge, Kabbalah, and the Book of Daniel," below: 63–77.
5. *Annual Review*, 23 (Jan. 1795): 92.
6. Nigel Leask, *Coleridge and the Politics of the Imagination* (London: Macmillan, 1988): 19–33. Leask persuasively argues that Coleridge's Unitarian interests mediate between his theory of the "One Life" and the politics of the Commonwealthsmen. Leask provides an excellent treatment of the influence of Harrington's ideas on Coleridge yet does not mention the role of Burgh here, nor does he discuss *The Plot Discovered* in this context. For Harrington's influence on Wordsworth see, Erdman, "Milton! Thou Shouldst Be Living," *TWC* 19 (1988): 2–8. Erdman, however, does not deal with Coleridge's reading of the Commonwealthsmen. See also *The Early Wordsworthian Milieu: A Notebook of Christopher Wordsworth with a Few Entries by William Wordsworth*, ed. Zera S. Fink (Oxford: Clarendon P., 1958), 107–17; and Zera S. Fink, *The Classical Republicans: An Essay in the Recovery of a Pattern of Thought in Seventeenth-Century England*, Northwestern University Studies in the Humanities 9 (Evanston, 1945).
7. Marilyn Butler, *Romantics, Rebels and Reactionaries* (Oxford: O.U.P., 1981): 81, 77–87.
8. See, Albert Goodwin, *The Friends of Liberty: The English Democratic Movement in the Age of the French Revolution* (London: Hutchinson, 1979): 361. Further references to this work will be cited in the main text as *Goodwin*. "Memoir of Thomas Hardy" (1832); reprinted in *Testaments of Radicalism: Memoirs of Working Class Politicians*, ed. D. Vincent (London: Europa, 1977): 37–102 (70).
9. Roe, *Wordsworth and Coleridge*, 156.
10. Carl B. Cone, *The English Jacobins, reformers in late 18th century England* (New York: Charles Scribner's Sons, 1968): 213.
11. John Thelwall, *Peaceful Discussion, and not tumultary violence, the means of redressing national grievance. The speech of J. Thelwall at the general meeting of the friends of parliamentary Reform, called by the London Corresponding Society, and ... held October 26, 1795*, 2nd edn. (London, 1795): 3–14.
12. E. P. Thompson, *The Making of the English Working Class* (Harmondsworth:

Penguin, 1968): 158; Henry Collins, "The London Corresponding Society," in *Democracy and the Labour Movement*, ed. John Savile (London: Lawrence & Wishart, 1955): 127; Roe, *Wordsworth and Coleridge*, 148–9.
13. P.A. Brown, *The French Revolution in English History* (London: 1918 [reprinted Frank Cass, 1965]): 152–4.
14. Thompson, *The Making of the English Working Class*, 159.
15. For the dating of the work see Peter J. Kitson, "Coleridge's *The Plot Discovered*: A New Date," *NQ* 31 (1984): 57–8.
16. For Harrington's influence, see Leask, *Politics of Imagination*, 34–45.
17. Blair Worden, *The Rump Parliament 1648–1653* (Cambridge: C.U.P., 1974): 40, 33–60, 172–7. See also David Underdown, *Pride's Purge: Politics in the Puritan Revolution* (Oxford: Clarendon P., 1971): 281–3.
18. Toby Barnard, *The English Republic 1649–1660*, Seminar Studies in History (Harlow: Longman, 1982): 66, 95.
19. See, Erdman, "Milton! Thou Shouldst Be Living," *TWC* 19; Fink (ed.), *The Early Wordsworthian Milieu*, 107–17.
20. James Holstun, *A Rational Millennium: Puritan Utopias of Seventeenth-Century England and America* (Oxford: O.U.P., 1987): 252, 260.
21. Christopher Hill, *Puritanism and Revolution: Studies in Interpretation of the English Revolution of the 17th Century* (London: Secker & Warburg, 1958): 50–122 (57). Further references to this work will be cited as *Hill* and contained in the text.
22. Milton identifies the Conquest as one of the "five bloody Inundations" leading to "Antichristian thraldome" (*MPW* 1:614).
23. The contest could not long be doubtful between a free nation, fierce in the enthusiasm of a warlike superstition, and the timid slaves of Rome, accustomed to crouch beneath every libertine or tyrant that oppressed them. (*Watchman*, 89–92)
24. W.H. Terry, *The Life and Times of John Lord Finch* (London, 1936): 571–2. Cited by Hill, 70.
25. *Reliquae Baxterianae*: 1: 51. Cited Hill, 71–2.
26. *Clarke Papers*, 2: 218. Cited Hill, 84.
27. It is unlikely that Coleridge or Southey actually encountered the writings of Winstanley first hand, although the leading ideas of his thought were available. Recently Iain McCalman has drawn attention to the currency of Winstanley's ideas among the followers of Thomas Spence; *Radical Underworld: Prophets, Revolutionaries and Pornographers in London, 1795–1840* (Cambridge: C.U.P., 1988): 64, 68, 71.
28. Gerrard Winstanley, *The True Levellers Standard Advanced* (1649), *Works*, ed. G. H. Sabine (Ithaca; Cornell U.P., 1941): 259. Hill, 85–6.
29. This anonymous essay has been variously attributed. Caroline Robbins, *The Eighteenth-Century Commonwealthman* (Cambridge, Mass.: Harvard U.P., 1959), 363–4, attributes it to Obadiah Hulme and Goodwin follows, 50–1; Patton and Mann and most commentators attribute it, probably wrongly, to the younger Allan Ramsay (1713–84); (*LPR* 305n). Hill leaves it as anonymous: Hill, 95–6. Coleridge and Burgh cite it merely by title.
30. See also Robbins, *Eighteenth-Century Commonwealthman*, 364.
31. John Thelwall, *The Rights of Nature against the Usurpations of Establishments. A Series of Letters addressed to the people of Britain, on the state of public affairs, and the recent effusions of the Rt. Hon. Edmund Burke. Letter the First*, 3rd edn. (London, 1976): 115–16.
32. Erdman, "Milton! Thou Shouldst Be Living," *TWC* (1988), 3.
33. George Whalley, "The Bristol Library Borrowings of Southey and Coleridge, 1793–98," *Library: Transactions of the Bibliographical Society*, fifth series, 4 (1949): 114–31. Coleridge borrowed the first two volumes in his own name and signed for Joseph Cottle for the third.
34. For Burgh see, Gilbert Cahill, "James Burgh," in *Biographical Dictionary of British Radicals Since 1770*, vol. 1: *1770–1832*, ed. J.O. Baylen and N.J. Gossman

"The electric fluid of truth" 61

(Brighton: Harvester P., 1979): 72–4; Robbins, *Eighteenth-Century Commonwealthman*, 364–8; Goodwin, 53–5; Oscar and Mary Handlin, "James Burgh and American Revolutionary Theory," *Proceedings of the Massachusetts Historical Society* 73 (1961): 38–57; Carla H. Hay, "The Making of a Radical: The Case of James Burgh," *The Journal of British Studies* 18 (1979): 90–117. See also Vernon W. Crane, "The Club of Honest Whigs: Friends of Science and Liberty," *William and Mary Quarterly*, 3rd series, 23 (1966); 210–33; Eugene Black, *The Association: British Extraparliamentary Political Organization, 1769–1793* (Cambridge, Mass.: Harvard U.P., 1963).

35. Crane, "The Club of Honest Whigs."
36. Milton's view of the desirability of shorter parliaments was to change over the years until in *The Readie & Easie Way* he argues for the permanency of his proposed Grand Council. For this development see, Z.S. Fink, "The Theory of the Mixed State and the Development of Milton's Political Thought," PMLA 57 (1942): 705–36.
37. See Worden's account, *The Rump Parliament*, 334–41.
38. For the influence of this on Coleridge's millenarianism, see Kitson, "Coleridge, Milton and the Millennium" *TWC* 17 (1987): 61–6. J.L. Lowes, *The Road to Xanadu* (Boston, 1927 [reprinted Bungay: Picador, 1968]): 316–17, gives Thomas Otway's *Venice Preserv'd: or a Plot Discovered* (1682) as the probable source of the phrase. Otway's play, however, does have an anti-Whig bias and it was a favourite with Pitt's government. Werkmeister, "Coleridge's *The Plot Discovered*: Some Facts and a Speculation," 254, refers to a loyalist handbill *The Downfal of Jacobinism, or the Plot Discovered* as a source.
39. Whalley, "Bristol Library Borrowings," 120.
40. Gilbert Burnet, *The History of His Own Times*, 2 vols. (London, 1724–34): 1: 543–4.
41. For the Bishop of Rochester's statement and the Earl of Lauderdale's reply, see the Debate in the Lords on the Treasonable Practices Bill, 11 Nov. 1795, in *The Parliamentary History of England*, ed. William Cobbett and John Wright, 36 vols. (London, 1806–20): 22: 257–8.
42. Burnet, *History*, 1: 544; for Rumbold, see *Biographical Dictionary of British Radicals in the Seventeenth Century*, ed. R.L. Graves and R. Zaller, 3 vols. (Brighton: Harvester P., 1982): 2: 118–19.
43. *PD* 1: 3; Burnet, *History*, 1: 633–4; Rumbold's words were, "I am sure there was no man born marked of God above another; for none comes into the world with a saddle on his back, neither any booted and spurred to ride him." *A Complete Collection of State Trials*, ed. T.B. and T.J. Howell, 33 vols. (London, 1809–26): 11: 873–81 (880).
44. *An Anatomy of the Lords Tyranny and iniustice exercised upon Lieu. Col. John Lilburne, now a prisoner in the Tower of London* (1646): 14–15. Thomas N. Corns, *English Political Literature, 1640–1660*, forthcoming.
45. For Thelwall and Coleridge, see Nicholas Roe, *Wordsworth and Coleridge*, 145–98; idem., "Coleridge and John Thelwall: The Road to Nether Stowey," in *Coleridge Connection*, 60–80; Peter J. Kitson, "Coleridge's Anecdote of John Thelwall," *NQ* 32 (1985): 345.
46. Debate in the Lords on the Treasonable Practices Bill, 6 Nov. 1795: *The Parliamentary History of England*, 22: 245, 248, 253.
47. Coleridge's source is *PD* 1: 120–1. Coleridge would also know of the details of Charles II's severity from the second chapter of Burnet's *History*.
48. Not everyone accepted Milton and Coleridge's equation of the voice of the people with the voice of God. Samuel Johnson provides a less elevated picture in *The False Alarm* (1770):

> The progress of the petition is well known. An ejected placeman goes down to his county or his borough, tells his friends of his inability to serve them, and his constituents of the corruption of the government. His friends readily under-

> stand that he who can get nothing, will have nothing to give. They agree to proclaim a meeting, meat and drink are plentifully provided ... Ale and clamour unite their powers, the crowd, condensed and heated, begins to ferment with the leaven of sedition. All see a thousand evils, though they cannot show them, and grow impatient for a remedy, though they know not what.

The Yale Edition of the Works of Samuel Johnson, ed. Donald J. Green, vol. 10 (New Haven; Yale U.P., 1977): 336–7.

49. Wylie, *Young Coleridge*, 110–11.
50. John Thelwall, *The Tribune*, 3 vols. (London, 1795), 3: 259.
51. Coleridge's satire on William Windham's use of language (*LPR* 286, 294) appears to have influenced John Thelwall's attack on Windham in *Sober Reflections on the Seditious and Inflammatory Letter to the Right Honourable Edmund Burke to a Noble Lord* (London, 1796), 7:

> what shall we say to "acquitted felons," "killed off" and a variety of other sentences, of whose "vitality" this subtle, Machiavellian secretary (terrified by the lingering echo of his own frenzy) has so pathetically complained?

52. Colmer, *Coleridge: Critic of Society*, 20.
53. Laura Lunger Knoppers, "Milton's *The Readie and Easie Way* and the English jeremiad," in *Politics, Poetics and Hermeneutics in Milton's Prose*, ed. David Loewenstein and James Grantham Turner (Cambridge: C.U.P., 1990): 213–25 (213–14). See also James Holstun, *A Rational Millennium*, 246–65. I am also indebted to Thomas N. Corns's discussion of this question in *English Political Literature, 1640–60*, forthcoming.
54. Knoppers, "Milton's Readie and Easie Way," 214.
55. James Holstun, *A Rational Millennium*, 253.
56. S.T. Coleridge, "College Commemoration Sermon," *BL*, Add. MSS, 34, 343: 31–64. The sermon has been partially transcribed by John Colmer, "An Unpublished Sermon of S.T. Coleridge," *NQ* 5 (1958): 150–2.

Coleridge, Kabbalah, and the Book of Daniel

INTRODUCTION

The status of scripture was a central question for Coleridge throughout his intellectual life. Much of his thought on the subject focused on the nature of prophecy, and it is this thought I shall be investigating here. In particular, the book of Daniel occupied Coleridge's mind in ways which caused him to change his religious and political views. I shall be tracing this change, suggesting that Coleridge developed a spiritual politics based on a new theory of scriptural interpretation, and that this theory owed much to the Jewish Kabbalah.

THE DECREES OF GOD

When, in a lecture of 1795, Coleridge cited the prophecies of Daniel, he was using the Old Testament in a way which was characteristic of his times. Taking the text as God's word he used it to show that Scripture includes divinely decreed predictions of the coming of a spiritual Messiah. He criticised the Jews who ignored the evidence of their own prophetic writing, and treated that writing as literally true and accurate. Taking as his text Daniel, Chapter 9: 24–7 Coleridge stated:

> the next Prophecy is still more remarkable – its authenticity never doubted – all the Jews, who have rejected Christ, believe the genuineness of the Book and that it was written by Daniel in the first year of Darius, about 500 years before the birth of Jesus. "Seventy weeks are determined upon thy People, and upon thy holy City, to finish the Transgression and to make an end of the Sin, and to make reconciliation for Iniquity. Know therefore, and understand, that from the going forth of the Commandment to restore and to build Jerusalem unto the Messiah the Prince shall be 7 weeks and threescore and two weeks. The streets shall be built again and the Wall, even in troublous Times. And after three-score and two weeks shall Messiah be cut off, but not for himself; and the People of the prince that shall come, shall destroy the city & the Sanctuary; and unto the end of the War Desolations are determined. And he shall confirm the Covenant with many for one week, and in the midst of the week he shall cause the Sacrifice and the Oblation to cease." In all the prophetical Writings a day is uniformly put for a year, and if we compute 72 weeks by this rule, we shall find then 504 years – the exact time that intervened between Daniel and Jesus. That the Messiah should be cut off

was directly opposite to the belief of the Jews – they therefore endeavoured to interpret the text figuratively, but so lamely, that the best Commentators regarded the passage as mysterious, till the Event proved that the Decrees of God are not regulated by the expectations of Men. (*LPR* 155)

Coleridge's distrust of figurative interpretation is noticeable, as is the blithe confidence with which he accepts the literal accuracy of his numerical computations. He stands firmly within the typological tradition, reading the Old Testament retrospectively to discover in it divine intimations of the truths announced in the New.

Coleridge, as the editors of his lectures for the *Collected Coleridge* have noted, was participating in a debate of great longevity in the eighteenth century, the debate over the evidences for Christianity (*LPR* 152n). Fulfilment of a prophecy was evidence of its truth, and the longer the period between prophecy and fulfilment, the stronger evidence it gave. If it was fulfilled after the Scriptures had been finished there could be no question of retrospective rewriting of the Old Testament so that it corruptly prophesied after the event. In taking this view Coleridge sided with his friend J.P. Estlin, a Unitarian minister in Bristol, against Thomas Paine, whose *Age of Reason* had treated prophecies as forgeries and poetic rhapsodies in its general attack on the Bible. The word "prophesy," wrote Paine, is used in a way that "strips it of all religious meaning, and shews that a man might then be a *prophet*, or he might *prophesy*, as he may now be a poet, or a musician."[1] There is some irony in the spectacle of Coleridge defending prophecy against claims that it is poetry, but he did so in line with his hero Priestley and his friend Estlin, whose pamphlet he may have helped to compose.[2] Estlin, in fact, praised the internal inconsistencies that Paine had attacked, claiming that "in all accounts given by eye witnesses, these circumstantial inconsistencies will appear. They are in themselves a very strong proof of the truth of the principal facts."[3]

Coleridge, himself a preacher in Unitarian chapels, could not afford to dispense with external evidences for Christianity or to accept that the internal evidence provided by Scripture was, as Paine claimed, a mixture of secular poetry and "trash."[4] And there was more than one reason why Coleridge could not do so. As a political radical, accused of Jacobinism and pro-French views, Coleridge had similar political hopes to Paine's. But Coleridge's religious radicalism consisted not of Paine's deistical natural religion, but of a move to Unitarianism that cost him a possible career in the Church of England – the career his revered father had followed. As a Unitarian Coleridge was dependent on a particular reading of the Bible that denied Christ's incarnate divinity. He therefore needed its authority, as did his dissenting lecture audiences, to support his refusal of the Trinitarian traditions of the established church. Paine's attacks on its status as God's word were, in fact, more dangerous to the Unitarians than to the Church of England, since the latter had centuries of tradition and practice to rely upon.

Paine was still more dangerous because, in linking political with religious change, he left fellow supporters of French innovations open to charges of irreligion and atheism:

> Soon after I had published the pamphlet COMMON SENSE, in America, I saw the exceeding probability that a revolution in the System of Government would be followed by a revolution in the System of Religion. The adulterous connection of church and state, wherever it has taken place, whether Jewish, Christian or Turkish, has so effectually prohibited, by pains and penalties, every discussion upon established creeds, and upon first principles of religion, that until the system of government should be changed, those subjects could not be brought fairly and openly before the world: but that whenever this should be done, a revolution in the system of religion would follow. Human inventions and priestcraft would be detected: and man would return to the pure, unmixed and unadulterated belief of one God, and no more.[5]

The Unitarians, mostly middle-class, were themselves campaigning for reform that would allow them and other dissenters to take public office. But to destroy biblical authority, as much as to support political revolution as England moved to war with France, would have been to ensure that their campaign was lost by association with treasonable atheism. Paine had, after all, been charged with sedition. Coleridge attacked Paine, writing that he saw the world as "a chaos of unintelligibles," and supported the reply of the establishment against him – "The Bishop of Llandaff has answered Payne" (*LPR* 150; *CL* 1: 193).

Defence of the authority of prophecy was necessary for rhetorical purposes of Coleridge's own. If he was sure of its reliability he could use its words in his own political preaching. The passage from Daniel quoted above allows Coleridge to make implicit allusions to political and moral degeneracy in contemporary England, suggesting by association that it warrants Jesus' return:

> At the time prophecied Jesus was born. The state of the Jewish and Gentile kingdoms was such as made his then coming more particularly seasonable. The age was more wicked and abandoned than any upon record – As to the Jews both their magistracy & Ministry were then corrupted to the last Degree. Riches gave impunity to the worst Villainy: their most sacred offices, whether in the Senate or the Priesthood were set to Sale ... (*LPR* 155)

The millenarian expectation of the second coming and the new Jerusalem was particularly powerful at this time, and Daniel was a particularly apposite text. However, whereas Richard Brothers believed his own predictions so literally that he declared himself God's nephew, Coleridge used prophecy as a critical strategy. Prophetic words gave his discourse authority and power, and by placing political matters in religious terms allowed him to appeal to piety rather than party for a spiritual renewal. Using biblical texts also kept the lecturer clear of charges of sedition, an important point as the government passed acts restricting free speech. Above all it gave the radicals the high moral ground by showing that their political ideas coincided with the truths expressed by God's prophets. In his journal *The Watchman* Coleridge castigated government ministers by quoting from Isaiah, "The Lord standeth up to plead. O my people, they, who lead thee, cause thee to err. The Lord will enter into judgment with the Princes ..." (*Watchman* 242). In poetry too Coleridge deployed prophecies to give his own voice a borrowed authority, semi-divine. Daniel and the Apocalypse come together in a millenarian vision of divine destruction and remaking which follows and punishes the destructions of the reformers' hopes by "Statesmen blood-stained and priests idolatrous":[6]

> ... Angels shout, Destruction! How his arm
> The last great Spirit lifting high in air
> Shall swear by Him, the ever-living One,
> Time is no more!
>
> Believe thou, O my soul,
> Life is a vision shadowy of Truth;
> And vice, and anguish, and the wormy grave,
> Shapes of a dream! The veiling clouds retire,
> And lo! the Throne of the redeeming God
> Forth flashing unimaginable day
> Wraps in one blaze earth, heaven, and deepest hell.
> (*PW* I: 124; *Religious Musings* lines 392–401)

At this point, one might argue, Coleridge has effectively conceded Paine's argument that prophecy is poetry rather than divine decree, for he is using scripture as a resource for his own poetic visions. However, to do so would be to miss the point that for this verse to be taken seriously, as Coleridge intended it to be and as it was, prior belief in the decreed truth of the scriptural texts on which it is based is necessary. Coleridge adapted prophetic words to suggest that the conditions required for the fulfilment of that prophecy were being met in his time, an adaptation of little import if writer and reader do not accept the prophecy as the word of God.

Acceptance, or the lack of it, is of course the crux for this kind of discourse. Coleridge's prophecies in prose and in poetry depend for their rhetorical power upon belief in the text whose authority they borrow. The figurative is thus peculiarly in thrall to the literal and needs to be defended against attacks upon it. Coleridge's attack on Paine's claim that prophecy is poetry is paradoxically a defence of his own prophetic poetry. The debate about evidences was not simply a continuation of an age-old controversy but a search for authority in politics and poetry at a time when both were in crisis.

THE SPIRIT IN THE LETTER

Coleridge's search for authority through prophetic evidences can be contrasted with Blake's, for whereas the poet of "Jerusalem" redefined the terms he borrowed in a personal mythology of visions, the religious muser remained uneasily dependent on them. It was probably his awareness of this that prevented him from writing his projected epic poem on the fall of Jerusalem.[7] After "Religious Musings" Coleridge began to find his reliance on a prophetic voice dangerous and restricting. It was dangerous because it tempted him into a bombastic association of himself with the Hebrew prophet; it was restricting because it depended on writer and audience sharing a literal belief in prophecy. As his dissenting audience dissolved, and as his own political and religious views changed, Coleridge found this belief disappear. This process was long and painful, too long to be detailed in this article, but, as Shaffer has shown, it involved exposure to German biblical criticism as well as disillusionment with political radicalism and an emotional need for Trinitarianism.[8] The study of Robert Lowth and Eichhorn, in particular, showed Coleridge a way of endorsing prophecy as poetry, without drawing Paine's inference that it was therefore uninspired and unreliable.[9] Coleridge, in fact, went further than either Lowth or Eichhorn by suggesting that a prophet was possessed by visions which he consciously re-possessed by developing them into poetic forms. Visions themselves were unconscious, but their nature was formed by the cultural experience and expectations of the seer; they were then reshaped by art. Prophecy was no longer divine decree, it was a mythologisation of unconscious apprehensions by conscious art, for the benefit of the spiritual direction of a people. Thus literal dictation and fulfilment were less important than the renewal of spiritual traditions in a language powerful enough to legislate for the future. On the one hand this was close to Coleridge's view of poetic genius – he praised Shakespeare for his conscious harnessing of the unconscious; on the other, it provided him with a new basis for a spiritual politics.

Coleridge's new spiritual politics was conservative in that it looked to tradition, but daring in that it saw the scripture on which that tradition was founded as mythological, rather than literal, in its expression of human intimations of the divine. Again he used Daniel as his text, but in a new way and for different reasons. Since these reasons have hardly been examined by critics, I wish to analyse them here. Daniel, Coleridge wrote, gave

> a lofty exhortation to his countrymen to spiritualize their Religion, to find the *Spirit* of individual morality in the *Letter* of their civil, and National Law – and in the genius of Pythagoras and Plato

coloured and shaped by ancestral Traditions and Hopes, by Hebraic and oriental imagery to sketch out a state, that should represent the whole internal perfected *Humanity* in expansion, i.e. in the form of the Many as One. (*NB* 54: 6)

The conjunction here of Pythagoras, Plato, Hebraic and oriental traditions is, at first sight, strange. Examination of Coleridge's other writings on this subject, however, reveals that he entertained the possibility that an oral tradition of patriarchal lore was passed down amongst the Hebrews and Egyptians. In *Aids To Reflection* he speculated that this lore was preserved as an inner meaning in Egyptian hieroglyphs, known only to priestly initiates. Mistranslation of these may have led to the Genesis account (*AR* 251–2). Scripture here had become a distorted reflection of a prior oral knowledge, and it therefore had to be read as symbolic of spiritual tradition. In his *Philosophical Lectures* Coleridge considered the possibility that this tradition might have been passed from priests – even from Ezekiel – to Pythagoras on the latter's trip to the East (*PL* 98). From this position he could, as did the German philosophers whom he had read, suggest that Greek neo-Platonism also contained fragments of patriarchal lore.[10]

How did the book of Daniel apply this lore? Coleridge gave some clues to his views in a letter of 1818, wondering whether "parts at least even of the five concluding chapters had not been tampered with by the commencing school of the Cabalists" (*CL* 4: 803). The Kabbalah was, in Coleridge's opinion, a pre-Christian Jewish tradition which fused Hebrew and Pythagorean fragments of patriarchal lore. The Alexandrian Jews, with their access to Jewish and Greek philosophy were, he wrote, "the Founders or Conservators of the Cabalistic Philosophy" (*NB* 36: 35^v). Elsewhere he stated that "the first and incorrupt period of the Cabala" recognised the Messiah as the Logos "before the apostolic age" (*NB* 41: 41). In avowing this Coleridge was historically applying knowledge that had long been available to him from his reading of contemporary theology and Renaissance philosophy. Bishop Bull, in a work Coleridge much admired, found Philo and the apostles to be the inheritors of the Kabbalah, whilst Basnage had stated in his *History of the Jews* that it "must have been already advanc'd into a Science in Philo's and our Lord's time."[11] Coleridge's lectures and notes display his knowledge of the use made of it in Renaissance neo-Platonism by Reuchlin, Pico, and Agrippa to portray the emanation of the Logos from God.[12]

Although he was occasionally critical of its pantheism (more often in public than in private where he was less afraid of seeming heretical), Coleridge was deeply indebted to the Kabbalah. His Christian reading of it saw it as an anticipation of Christ the Word in the heart of Jewish scripture. This suggested that the Logos was not a post-Christ neo-Platonist imposition upon Jesus but a conception native to the Jews and one, moreover, descended from a patriarchal lore reflected in many oriental traditions. The Kabbalah was, for Coleridge, the tradition in which the others met and as such was a vital confutation of the Unitarianism he had formerly practised and evidence of the recurring and universal mental necessity to think of God in terms of Logos. Coleridge was looking for, and was satisfied he had found, historical evidence of the a priori necessity of Trinitarian belief:

> Paul's writings seem to me already to prove, that a spiritual Conception of the Messiah, & of his communion with the Soul, was entertained by some at least of the Doctors between the Return from the Captivity & the Birth of our Lord. (*NB* 47: 19^v)

Paul, as we shall see, echoed Daniel.

The kabbalism present in Daniel consisted, in Coleridge's opinion, of an "interior sense," one symbolised by the letter of the Jewish law indicating the coming of a spiritual redeemer, not a military leader, as Messiah. The last five chapters of Daniel contain several passages which could be regarded as kabbalistic. Of these the lengthiest appears at Dan. 7: 14:

> And there was given him dominion, and glory, and a kingdom, that all people, nations, and languages should serve him: his dominion is an everlasting dominion, which shall not pass away, and his kingdom that which shall not be destroyed.

Passages at Dan. 4: 3, 4: 34, and 7: 27 also make use of "glory," "kingdom" and "dominion." As Coleridge recognised, these words, as well as "splendour," were names of the *sephiroth*, the kabbalistic emanations of God. They are detailed in the major text of kabbalism, *The Zohar*, which Coleridge knew through his friendship with the Hebrew scholar Hyman Hurwitz and its translation in *Kabbala Denudata*.[13] According to *The Zohar* and *Sepher Jetzirah* (also known to Coleridge) God, himself unknowable, withdrew into himself to create a point.[14] From this the sephiroth, emanations, were produced, creating the Torah and the world. The sephiroth were expressed as a progression of lights, but also as a progression of names and letters. As lights and names they progressed from the first sephira, *kether*, the crown, into a total of ten, the second of which was *chochmah*, "wisdom," the eighth *hod*, "splendour/glory," the last, in which all ten were summed *malkuth* "bride/kingdom." Divine names associated with them were *Yah*, representing wisdom, *Tzabaoth*, representing victory and glory, *Adonai*, representing kingdom.[15] As letters, the sephiroth expanded from three "mother" letters into ten, and from ten into the twenty-two consonants of the Hebrew alphabet.

Why was Coleridge excited about the presence of this arcane symbolism in Daniel? Because he, along with other Christian interpreters of kabbalism, saw the sephirothic system as establishing the doctrine of the Logos, and sketching out Trinitarianism. The sephiroth showed God's creative energy to be *verbal*; His world and His book were both language in which He was present. There was a danger of a pantheistic collapse of God into His creation here, which Coleridge acknowledged.[16] But Christian interpreters such as Pico and Henry More countered this by reading the second sephira, "wisdom," as Christ the Logos. They interpreted it as creative energy and saw its renewal in the tenth sephira *malkuth* as a prediction of Christ's return in glory in a redeemed "kingdom." Henry More, for instance, wrote in his book on Daniel of "Christ's Kingdom, the *Malcuth* of the God of *Israel*, which is the Tenth Sephirah with the *Cabbalists*."[17] This reading confirmed John's neo-Platonic description of Christ as the Logos, as Coleridge showed when he discussed kabbalistic names:

> Gloria ut Solis = Splendor sempiternè generatus: Praise, Sonus seu Verbum glorificans – all three titles of the Messiah, adopted by the Cabbalists, and used by St Paul. (*CM* 1: 438)

Coleridge's Latin, which translates as "a Glory as of the Sun = a Splendour eternally generated: Praise, a glorifying Sound or Word," links the relations of the sephiroth with those established by John's gospel between God and Christ, the Logos or Word. In John 1: 14 John has "the glory as of the only begotten of the Father."

The Trinitarian implications of the sephiroth were linked by Coleridge to the presence in Kabbalah of Pythagorean mathematics. In his *Philosophical Lectures* he talked of "the numbers of Pythagoras and the Cabalists" and explained how the sephiroth were based on the numbers three and seven:

> The Deity considered in himself and in his own essential nature they represented as three in one; but the Deity as manifested, as expanding in at least seven ways, they represented as the seven spirits or the seven Sephiroth. The last, which was to be the Messiah or the Shekinah, was to be the same as the second person of the triad, and to be in the Shekinah a concentration of all the seven spirits of the manifestation. (*PL* 115, 299)

The sephirothic system resembled the Pythagorean account of number, which indicated the generative power of numerical relations, from the first four units $(1 + 2 + 3 + 4)$ producing ten, and so potentially all number. Like the sephiroth, Pythagorean numbers could therefore be used to symbolise a creative mental energy or, as Coleridge concluded, "THE Reason itself in act" (*PL* 115). The appearance of the sephirothic names in Daniel, then, was of more than historical interest, for it not only indicated the presence of Jewish tradition, but alluded to a codification of creative energy that was supported by mathematics. Representing God and the Messiah in this way not only anticipated Christian Trinitarianism, then, but raised belief to philosophy. Coleridge wrote in a notebook that kabbalism "in it's primary and purist state deserved the name" of philosophy since it believed in "the Word, or the Name" (*NB* 36: 35^v).[18] Put more expansively, it deserved it not only for its belief in the name, but for its codification of the relations between names, between the divine name "I am" and all the other names that sprang from it, the human consciousness or "I am" included. To return to Coleridge's praise of Daniel, kabbalistic tradition found the spirit in the letter by showing letters (and numbers) to be the emanations of the One into Many.

KABBALISTIC HERMENEUTICS

In the manuscript "On the Divine Ideas" Coleridge wrote of his interest in the Kabbalah both for "historical evidence & still more for hermeneutic purposes as determining the true sense of the christian scriptures considered as historical documents."[19] This interest was, in fact, based on the traditional practice of kabbalists, although it was put to different use. The Kabbalah had always been an interpretative system as well as a doctrine: it not only declared that God emanated in words, but decoded the words of scripture to find their inner, divine, meaning. Coleridge was aware of the specialised techniques used, but preferred himself to discuss the issues that they raised. In so doing, he worked towards a new theory of prophecy that accepted the findings of German biblical critics. Prophecies could not be accepted as divinely dictated; their fulfilment by events described by the apostles in the New Testament could not be relied upon – the apostles might have concocted the evidence. However, the prophecies could be seen as kabbalistic, in which case they might be symbolic of an inner sense that possession of the kabbalists' hermeneutical methods would have revealed (and, perhaps, still could):

> I confess that the opinion of an interior spiritual sense, in the mind of the Prophets themselves, preserved for a time in the schools of the Prophets, and still discoverable by a spiritual light would be full of comfort to me, to remove difficulties which I at present see no other means of overcoming or even of escaping – if only I could be sure, it was more than an opinion. (The invidious epithets of Swedenborgian and Cabalistic would not frighten me.) (*NB* 35: 47ᵛ)

Coleridge hoped to discover the inner sense by inheriting fragments of the "esoteric doctrine" and hermeneutic passed down from the prophets and dimly mirrored in medieval and Renaissance mysticism (*NB* 52: 9). This was a hope unlikely to be satisfied, but it gave Coleridge the confidence to develop his notions of verbal symbolism beyond the Kabbalah to language in general, and thence to redefine conceptions of history and politics.

Daniel 7: 9 says of the Ancient of Days that "his throne was like the fiery flame, and his wheels as burning fire." Here the prophet's vision resembles Ezekiel's vision of the throne-chariot and its wheels. In his

Statesman's Manual Coleridge quoted Ezekiel's vision and made it into a definition of the symbol:

> *Whithersoever the Spirit was to go, the wheels went, and thither was their spirit to go: for the spirit of the living creature was in the wheels also.* The truths and the symbols that represent them move in conjunction and form the living chariot that bears up (for *us*) the throne of the Divine Humanity. (*LS* 29)

The ancient Jewish tradition of *merkabah*, "chariot," mysticism had been developed by Jewish kabbalists. Some saw the *ophanim*, "wheels," as the letters of God's name. The world of archetypes, of sephiroth of which all lower worldly things are shadows, was often termed *merkabah*; the lower world (the human one) was associated with the wheels.[20] The Christian Kabbalah, meanwhile, interpreted the figure on the chariot as the Logos, the spiritual Messiah.[21] Clearly, Coleridge was alluding to these traditions here. But, more important, he was using their interpretation of Ezekiel to define interpretative language. Their symbols were providing him with a theory of symbolism in which truth and its representative symbols are not separate, any more than in the Kabbalah God's creative words (Logos/ Word) and the words by which we interpret them are separate. Coleridge's notion of Christ as "the Divine Humanity" is a verbal one then, derived from kabbalistic doctrine and hermeneutics as well as from St John. He repeated the quotation from Ezekiel at the start of *Aids to Reflection*, using it to define a language of *"living* Words" (*AR* xi–xii).

If language is multiple, necessarily alluding to a unity from which it springs, then only a Word which combines unity with all potential multiplicity can fully reconcile the two. For Coleridge the Kabbalah had recognised that necessity, and found such a word. Christ the Logos, on this account, was a reconciling symbol required by language (and therefore human nature itself). The incarnation of the Logos as the historical Jesus completed this necessary symbol by enacting it as a living divine humanity. Coleridge continued to praise the kabbalists for conceiving this symbolic understanding of God as Word. Their interpretation of God's names revealed the spirit or *numen* present in them and all words, and should have redefined the historical relationship between the Jews and their Lord: "As the Filial Word to God, so should the whole of Israel have been to the Word, the Messiah – Messias diffusus – Nomen Dei, idem ac *Numen*, i.e. praesentia intelligibilis" [Messiah spread abroad – the Name of God, which is the same as his *Numen* – that is, his intelligible presence] (*CM* 1: 438).

In Coleridge's subsequent revision of Biblical history, prophecies become symbolic human narratives of man's linguistic relation to God. None is literal, or final, but the inner sense of each demonstrates in new terms the need for a uniting Word.[22] The Logos is symbolised in different human terms endlessly, but is seen always as a redeemer of society and history through language. In Coleridge's portrayal he, the inheritor of the hermeneutic of the inner sense, recreates this symbolisation, renews the sacred mythmaking, in his own interpretation. Just as his prophets become poets so he, poet turned biblical critic, performs in his interpretation the task he had once defined as that of the (poetic) imagination, "the repetition in the finite mind of the eternal act of creation in the infinite I AM (*BL* I: 305). "I am," of course, is a Hebrew name for God.

It is no surprise to find that, in *The Statesman's Manual*, Coleridge establishes his view of symbolic narratives with a discussion of a text which echoes the kabbalistic vocabulary found in Daniel. He quotes Paul's epistle to the Colossians.

> Who (viz. the Father) hath delivered us from the power of darkness and hath translated us into the kingdom of his dear Son: In whom we have redemption through his blood, even the forgiveness of sins: Who is the image of the invisible God, the first born of every creature: For by him were all things created, that are in heaven, and that are in earth, visible and invisible, whether they be thrones, or dominions, or principalities, or powers ... (*LS* 44)

Daniel, of course, contained the phrase "Son of Man" as well as the names thrones, dominions and powers. It was traditional to treat the phrase as a prophecy of Christ, realised in the New Testament as here in Paul. Coleridge's interpretation was different, however. He noticed that Daniel referred not to the "Son of Man," but "*one* like the Son of man": "behold, *one* like the Son of Man came with the clouds of heaven" (Daniel 7: 13). The word "like" indicated that Daniel did not see the Messiah *as* the Son of Man, but meant by the phrase "the semblance of a human form" only. Daniel was not a literally true prophecy of the Messiah–Son then, but had been retrospectively read as such by those of Jesus' time.

> Yet that this Text might have OCCASIONED the use of this phrase to designate the Messiah, is very possible – and in this view the adoption of the Name by the Jews contemporary with our Lord furnishes a strong argument against the Socinians. S.T.C. (*CM* 1: 441)

Daniel's symbolic account of his visions had been redefined by the needs of those contemporary with Christ to find a tradition supporting their recognition of him as God incarnate. Narratives were not only symbolic then, but subject to redefinition in history by the human need to show that history was an anticipation of current discoveries and ideas.

The very fact that Paul had alluded to Daniel in Colossians suggested to Coleridge that Paul had meant to portray Jesus as the Son of God and the Messiah anticipated by the Jews. In his *Statesman's Manual* Coleridge followed the quoted passage with a refutation of the "free-thinking" scepticism of critics who, like Eichhorn, thought it to "mean only" that Christ was the chief figure of the church, not necessarily of the universe (*LS* 44–5). Paul's symbolism could not be so easily dismissed. Nor, however, could it be easily accepted as a "mystery" requiring no enquiry into its meaning. Between scepticism and blind faith another path lay, a path along which a "previously re-generated" heart would lead enquirers "'to a full *assurance* of Understanding ..., (*to an entire assent of the mind; to a spiritual intuition, or positive inward knowledge by experience*) of the mystery of God, *and* of the Father, *and* of Christ'" (*LS* 46). This path began in faith, but proceeded through the acceptance of Scripture as a consciously shaped symbolic narrative, drawing deliberately on tradition to shape the individual prophet's vision in historically powerful terms. These terms, subjective as they now were, acquired new authority through the new use made of them, both in the prophet's narrative and the inquirer's interpretation of it. Paul had drawn deliberately on the kabbalistic traditions of Daniel to demonstrate that he meant more by his descriptions than Eichhorn suggests, for they show the Messiah as the Son and as sephirothic energy.

Coleridge was using Eichhorn's historical and textual criticism but surpassing it. Instead of seeing conscious manipulation of tradition as a mark of falsehood he saw it as evidence of the prophets' determination to share their personal visions in historically powerful symbols. No one account would be literally true, but together the prophecies formed a tradition of spiritual symbolism. Here Coleridge implied that the enquiring reader resembled the prophet-poets described by Bishop Lowth, reshaping in his understanding the narratives that they had consciously reshaped in accordance with their own understandings of God. Coleridge had salvaged conscious creativity in Scripture from the clutches of divine dictation on the one hand, secular fabrication on the other. In so doing he had opened the way to Newman's "grammar of assent," for the re-interpretation of others' interpretations led from symbols to faith.[23]

The Kabbalah retained its importance in this scheme since if subjective interpretation was not to become arbitrary it needed guidance from tradition. The Kabbalah was part of tradition, its symbolic terms and its theory of symbolism having been employed by the Old and New Testament writers. Just as Paul had reinvigorated it by adapting Daniel, so the modern interpreter could revive it as a personal but historical symbolism of God. Through the Kabbalah, then, Coleridge could participate in an "inner sense," a spiritual tradition which would both guide his interpretation and give him authority. In a late notebook he wrote that Greek myths display fancy, and the "patriarchal anticipation" of Christianity shows imagination (*NB* 50: 12^v). The "oral and traditional faith ... continued in the earliest Cabbala" now guided and supported the imagination which, in the *Biographia*, it had been the poet's lonely task to exercise (*NB* 53: 6).

PROPHECY AND POLITICS

Coleridge's confidence that he participated in the inner, spiritual interpretation of Scripture allowed him to re-enter political debate. Possession of the esoteric inner sense gave him rhetorical authority, for it aligned him with an ancient tradition of revered interpreters. Moreover, it founded his politics on an élite tradition of scriptural interpretation that was invulnerable to political attack. From this position Coleridge advocated spiritual reform as the basis of political change: it was a duty to reform oneself and to enable others to reform themselves by a spiritual understanding of Scripture. The unity of a Christian society was dependent on all its members being active interpreters of the Bible, and it was the duty of the higher and learned classes to ensure that this was possible for the lower and ignorant.

> To *make use* of all the means and appliances in our power to the actual attainment of Rectitude, is the abstract of the Duty which we owe to ourselves: To *supply* those means as far as we can, comprizes our Duty to others. The question then is, what are those means? Can they be any other than the communication of Knowledge and the removal of those Evils and Impediments which prevent its reception? It may not be in our power to combine both, but it is in the power of every man to contribute to the former, who is sufficiently informed to feel that it is his Duty. If it be said, that we should endeavor not so much to remove Ignorance, as to make the Ignorant religious: Religion herself, through her sacred oracles, answers for me, that all effective Faith presupposes Knowledge and individual Conviction. (*LS* 47)

Later, in *On the Constitution of the Church and State*, Coleridge proposed a clerisy, an institution of educators whose dissemination of spiritual understanding would reconcile social classes and interests, private and national property, and church and state. In doing so he invoked the Hebrew "institution of the *Nabim*, or Prophets ... protectors of the Nation and privileged state moralists" (*C&S* 38).

Coleridge's idealisation of the prophets was soon left behind by the changing politics and class relations of Victorian Britain. But it continued to influence ideas on culture, on education and on the role of the church. His revision of the status of prophecy, his emphasis on the role of human imagination in vision, poetry, and interpretation may be contrasted with the work of his British contemporaries. Edward Irving, the Scottish preacher whose sermons brought him fashionable success in the London of the 1820s, was influenced by Coleridge, and dedicated a book to him. But Irving's interpretation of the book of Daniel not only ignored the kabbalistic traditions and textual questions presented by it but made it the servant of a frustrated millenarianism. The "opening of the Millennial dispensation" could be expected within forty years, with

Christ returning in person as absolute ruler: "it is simply a universal kingdom that is given to him over all people, nations, and languages – that is all."[24] Irving's literalism was matched by James Hatley Frere who, however, fixed 1822–23 as the time in which Daniel would be fulfilled "by the overthrow of the Infidel power, the final destruction of the Papacy."[25] Coleridge wrote that Frere was "swallowed up in the quicksands of conjectural prophecy," regretted his influence on Irving, and publicly rejected both men's *"interpretations* of the Apocalypse and the Book of Daniel" (*CL* 4: 557, *C&S* 141). They ignored the "canons of Symbolic Poesy" as practised by the Hebrews, and they transferred their hopes for spiritual and political reform into predictions of the absolute rule of the Messiah (*C&S* 140n.).

It is to Coleridge's credit that he resisted spiritual politics such as Irving's, preferring to the conjectural millenarianism of his own youth an advocacy of symbolic narrative. Re-interpreting the prophets' interpretations of the divine placed knowledge in the interpreter's power, for in so doing he could symbolise spiritual truth anew. This symbolism was conservative in its emphasis on tradition, but characteristically innovative, in secular and religious politics, in making the creative interpretation of each Bible reader the means by which that tradition could renew the self and society. The Book of Daniel, including in itself the interpretations of the kabbalists and giving rise to the reinterpretations of Paul, was vital to that tradition and, in Coleridge's hands, vital to a new understanding of the writing of man, God, and history.

TIM FULFORD

NOTES

1. Thomas Paine, *The Age of Reason: Being an Investigation of True and Fabulous Theology* (Paris and London, 1794), 15.
2. Priestley endorsed prophecy as divine dictation in *An Answer To Mr. Paine's Age of Reason, Being a Continuation of Letters to the Philosophers and Politicians of France on the Subject of Religion; and of the Letters to a Philosophical Unbeliever* (London, 1795), 93. Peter J. Kitson discusses Coleridge's millenarian interpretation of prophecy in "Coleridge, Milton and the Millennium," *TWC* 18 (1987): 61–6.
3. J.P. Estlin, *Evidences of Revealed Religion and particularly Christianity stated, with reference to a Pamphlet called The Age of Reason* (Bristol, 1796), 52.
4. Paine, *Age of Reason*, 15.
5. Paine, *Age of Reason*, 2–3.
6. See Daniel 11: 6; Revelation 4: 2–5.
7. The poem's mythology would have been a "completion of the prophecies"; Coleridge added "I schemed at twenty-five; but, alas! *venturum expectat*" (28 April 1832: *TT*: 160).
8. E.S. Shaffer, *"Kubla Khan" and the Fall of Jerusalem* (Cambridge: Cambridge U.P., 1975), 22–95.
9. Lowth, *De Sacra Poesi Hebraeorum* (Oxford, 1753) was read by Coleridge in 1796. For a discussion of Lowth's influence on Coleridge's view of Hebrew poetry see Stephen Prickett, *Words and The Word: Language Poetics and Biblical Interpreta-*

tion (Cambridge: Cambridge U.P., 1986), 105–23. Eichhorn, influenced by Lowth, gave a course of lectures attended by Coleridge in Göttingen. For discussion of this see Shaffer, *Kubla Khan* 23; for Coleridge's later marginalia on Eichhorn see *CM* 2: 369–520.

10. F.W.J. Schelling, *Ueber die Gottheiten von Samothrace* (Stuttgart and Tübingen, 1815) discusses the presence of patriarchal lore in the Greek mysteries. For Coleridge's reaction to Schelling see *CM* 2: 573–85 and *Miscellaneous Criticism*, ed. T.M. Raysor (London: Constable, 1936), 192–3.

11. George Bull, *Defensio Fidei Nicaenae* (Oxford, 1851–2) I: 27–9; Jacques Basnage de Beauval, *The History of the Jews from Jesus Christ to the Present Time*, tr. Thomas Taylor (London, 1708), 206.

12. See *PL* 295–303, *CN* 3: 4497. See Tim Fulford, *Coleridge's Figurative Language* (London: Macmillan, forthcoming, 1990) for a detailed discussion of Coleridge's interest in the Kabbalah.

13. Coleridge met Hurwitz in Highgate, collaborated with him in poetry and relied on his knowledge of Hebrew; see *CL* 4: 784, 871. The *Kabbala Denudata* may have been amongst Coleridge's books whilst he was still in the Lake District; later it was in the library of J.H. Green, to whom many of Coleridge's books passed after his death. Christian Knorr von Rosenroth, *Kabbala Denudata* (Frankfurt, 1677–84).

14. Coleridge referred to *Sepher Jetzirah* in *CL* 5: 8. His knowledge of it may have come indirectly through discussions of it by Reuchlin, More, and Tenneman, the historian of philosophy. A Latin version was available in J. Pistorius, *Artis Cabalisticae* (Basle, 1587). On God's withdrawal into a point see Akiba Ben Joseph, *The Book of Formation (Sepher Yetzirah)*, tr. Knut Stenring (London: William Rider, 1923), 21–31 and *The Zohar*, translated from the Latin by S.L. Macgregor Mathers, *Kabbala Denudata: the Kabbalah Unveiled* (London, 1887), 268.

15. See Mathers, *Kabbalah Unveiled*, 88.

16. Coleridge's interest in the Kabbalah was tempered by his fear, especially strong in his public discourse, of seeming to endorse pantheism. In a lecture he called it a "species of pantheism" (*PL* 299) and in a note he remained cautious about its idea of the Trinity: "I do not say that there is not a great deal of truth in this; but I say that it is not, as the Cabalists represent it, the whole truth." See *Literary Remains*, ed. E.H. Coleridge (London, 1836–39), 4: 319.

17. Henry More, *A Plain and Continued Exposition of the Several Prophecies or Divine Visions of the Prophet Daniel* (London, 1681), 78. Giovanni Pico della Mirandola, *Opera Omnia* (Basle, 1557–73, reprint Hildesheim; Georg Olms, 1969), I: 111.

18. Although modern scholars accept that the Kabbalah is of medieval, rather than pre-Christian, date they accept that Jewish belief in the power of the holy name is of much earlier origin. See G.G. Scholem, *On the Kabbalah and Its Symbolism* (New York: Schocken, 1969), 37–8 and compare Origen, "Against Celsus" in *The Writings of Origen*, tr. F. Crombie (Edinburgh and London, 1869–72), I: 421–3.

19. "On the Divine Ideas," ms. in the Henry E. Huntington Library, San Marino, California, 157.

20. Scholem, *On the Kabbalah*, 124.

21. Knorr von Rosenroth, *Kabbala Denudata*, I: 184.

22. Coleridge may have acquired his belief in an inner sense from Henry More, who suggested that Scripture contained a "*Spiritual sense*," a Kabbalah or "Traditionary Doctrine" known to the prophets and passed by them to Pythagoras. See *The Defence of the Threefold Cabbala*, 54 in *A Collection of Several Philosophical Writings* (London, 1712).

23. On Coleridge's contribution to Newman's and other modern hermeneutics see *The Context of English Literature: The Romantics*, ed. Stephen Prickett (London: Methuen, 1981), 155–9.

24. Edward Irving, *The Church and State Responsible to Christ, and to One Another* (London, 1829), 516, 486–7.

25. James Hatley Frere, *A Combined View of the Prophecies of Daniel, Esdras, and St. John* (London, 1815), 200.

"Murdering One's Double": De Quincey's "Confessions of an English Opium Eater" and S.T. Coleridge's "Biographia Literaria"

Contemporary critical neglect of De Quincey's *Confessions of an English Opium Eater*, a work which addressed the issues of compulsion and dependence in a challenge to what its author considered as the flawed voluntarism of the "High Romantic argument," is perhaps all the more remarkable given the deconstructive mood of so much recent revisionary work on English romanticism. Perhaps this is partly because De Quincey's book has always stood in a somewhat uneasy relationship to the literary canon; it took the drug culture of the 1960s, rather than any swing of literary mood, to reawaken an interest in De Quincey, an interest which is manifest in Alethea Hayter's 1968 study *Opium and the Romantic Imagination* and a first Penguin edition of the *Confessions* in 1971.

Although De Quincey's title evokes the autobiographical *Confessions* of St Augustine and Jean-Jacques Rousseau, he was at pains to declare that the subject of his book was impersonal, "preternatural," pharmaceutical, rather than autobiographical, natural, or spiritual. "Not the opium-eater but the opium is the true hero of the tale: and the legitimate centre on which the interest revolves," he wrote in the *Confessions* (DQC 114). When De Quincey added extensive autobiographical material to the work's 1856 *rifacciamento*, the mild disappointment felt by many readers was expressed by Henry Crabb Robinson, who wrote "It is delightful, but it is now become more autobiographical ...."[1] Initial reception of the 1821 *London Magazine* articles which were republished in book form in 1823 had been in general positive, although it is clear that most of the fifteen early reviewers tended to read it as a medical account of opium addiction and an intervention in a current debate about the therapeutic value of opium rather than as a work of independent literary merit. From the beginning, however, there was some uncertainty about the book's moral tendencies, perhaps understandable when one considers the "reader's response" to the *Confessions*, which make the tears shed over Richardson's *Clarissa* or Rousseau's *Nouvelle Héloïse* seem rather tame by comparison. The hyperaesthetic and hypnagogic vistas of the dreams with which De Quincey concluded (dreams which he declared to be "the real object of the whole" – *DQC* 126) appear to have caused many readers to experiment with opium. In 1823, at the inquest into the death of a young man who had overdosed on opium, the reporting doctor "claimed to have direct knowledge of four cases in which the patients, when questioned, gave [*The Confessions*] as their inspiration for taking a near-fatal dose."[2] De Quincey's friend John Wilson, in his "Noctes Ambrosianae" sketch in *Blackwood's Magazine* for October 1823, discussed the "fifty unintentional suicides" caused by the book, concluding, with characteristic glib humour, in the author's favour: only six had actually died, and this "only show[ed] the danger that dunces run into when they imitate men of genius."[3] Sensitive to the charge that his work contained "an overbalance on the side of the *pleasures* of opium," and not enough on the *pains* to act as a deterrent to would be opium-eaters, De Quincey in November 1821 promised the readers of the *London Magazine* a Third Part to remedy the situation (*DQC* 119–20). The fact that this was never written, and that the 1856 revision was unrepentant in its advocacy of the pleasures and therapeutic benefits of opium (it even urged insurance companies not to discriminate against opium dependants in transacting Life Insurance policies), reveals De Quincey's dogged belief in the drug's positive effects, despite his personal failure to "unwind the accursed chain" of addiction. It was upon the possibility of such a relinquishment that his advocacy of opium largely rested, a point to which I will return.

De Quincey's doggedness notwithstanding, the morbid "reader's response" to his book fuelled the arguments of its medical opponents. *The Family Oracle of Health*, for example, was of the opinion in January 1824 that "this wicked book" must be held responsible for the misery caused by "its lying stories about celestial dreams, and similar nonsense." "Drunkenness is not confined to the use of fermented liquors," it continued, "the tipplers of laudanum are sots, although of another sort."[4] Underlying the *Family Oracle*'s indignation was the argument of the naval surgeon Thomas Trotter's *Essay on Drunkenness* (1804), the first medical work to give pathological status to intoxication by alchohol and drugs. Although Trotter believed that opium had utility as a panacea for terminal illnesses, he regarded its habitual use as causing "debility, emaciation, loss of intellect, palsy, dropsy, dyspepsia, hepatic diseases and others which flow from the indulgence of spiritous liquors."[5] Like all the medical opponents of opium, Trotter believed that dependance upon opium, like that on alcohol, was unbreakable, a charge which De Quincey (despite personal evidence to the contrary) denied.[6] The *Confessions*, without mentioning Trotter, also denied his thesis that opium caused this impressive list of diseases, or that it could be described as an intoxicant at all. This latter point he argued against no less an authority than the leading contemporary surgeon of the day John Abernethy, himself a laudanum addict on 450 drops a day (an inconsiderable amount compared to De Quincey's 8 to 9,000 drops daily at his peak addiction period). Abernethy's error in supporting Trotter's argument, De Quincey concluded, was semantic, based on "the logical error of using the word intoxication with too great latitude, and extending it generically to all modes of nervous excitement, connected with certain diagnostics" (*DQC* 75). The fact that Abernethy, in a recent polemic with the radical surgeon William Lawrence, had defended a vitalist position against the atheism and French materialism he found implicit in Lawrence's theory is relevant to my argument here. In attacking Abernethy, De Quincey was also having a dig at Coleridge, whose *Essay on Scrofula* included a tribute to Abernethy and whose *Theory of Life* attacked Lawrence's definition of Life as a function of organisation rather than as a superinduced principle. De Quincey might have sought to discredit Trotter's arguments about intoxication, but on one count at least (which incidentally proves his knowledge of the uncited *Essay on Drunkenness*) he was willing to concede. Trotter was the source for the contemporary theory that intoxication caused spontaneous combustion, fear of which – the terrible fate which overtakes Krook the rag merchant in *Bleak House* – De Quincey tells us, in the 1856 *Confessions*, caused him seriously to attempt a reduction of his laudanum consumption. This attempt was contemporaneous with a bizarre story in the *Westmoreland Gazette* (of which De Quincey was editor in 1818 and 1819) about an "Incombustible Man," together with a recipe for an ointment of marshmallows, eggs and radishes with which concerned readers could fireproof their flesh as an alternative to relinquishing alchohol and drugs. Whatever Trotter's medical errors, the opium-eater wasn't taking any chances on this one.[7]

Trotter's *Essay on Drunkenness* preferred the well-tried "opiates of the soul," "religious and moral sentiments," to more preternatural remedies.[8] In emphasising the narcotic and sedative, rather than the stimulating, effects of opium, and by presenting disease and dependence as pathological consequences of the drug, Trotter's work challenged a body of medical theory based on the teachings of the Edinburgh doctor John Brown (1735–88), known as the "Brunonian system." The title derived from Brown's Latin *Elementa Medicinae* (1780) which ensured the work great popularity on the continent, particularly in Germany and Italy. Reinterpreting the work of his mentor, William Cullen, Professor of Clinical Medicine at Edinburgh, Brown argued that the nervous system was composed of excitable tissue, highly sensitive (or "sensible") to its environment. As Christopher Lawrence has remarked of the eighteenth-century Scottish theorisation of the nervous system, the monistic and essentially materialist psychology which it developed implied that "all man's higher attributes – taste, imagination, and indeed the capacity to reason – would, in the last analysis, depend on his condition of existence, diet, weather, labour and so forth ... Sensibility, [was] in the end related to the individual's mode of life and should, in the healthy state, be properly adjusted to it."[9] Medicine was thus a preternatural means of resolving natural maladjustment. Brown classified all diseases as "sthenic" or "asthenic," according to whether they increased or decreased the state of excitement of the nervous tissue. For asthenic diseases (caused by understimulation), he recommended "stimulating remedies, in particular brisk exercise or opium"; he believed that most doctors, including Cullen, misunderstood the properties of opium: "instead of allowing it to be the strongest stimulant in nature, they made it a sedative ... Another property they ascribed to it was that of bringing on sleep: whereas, it is the most powerful body of all others in producing and keeping up the watchful state." The debate between the Brunonians and the Cullenites (as well as with the followers of F.J.V. Broussaise who advocated bloodletting by leeches, which, as Robert Woof has pointed out, is an important subtext to Wordsworth's "Leech Gatherer"[10]) survived into the beginning of the nineteenth century, although medical consensus increasingly lay with the Cullenites who accepted that the primary effect of opium was its narcotic rather than its stimulating influence on the system.

There is no doubt that De Quincey's *Confessions* is permeated with the increasingly unfashionable discourse of Brunonianism. "The primary effects of opium are always, in the highest degree, to excite and stimulate the system," he wrote in the section entitled "The Pleasures of Opium" (*DQC* 77). By the same token, he denied that the drug led, at least in his own highly refined nervous system, to "torpor and stagnation, animal and mental." Opium "greatly increase[s] the activity of the mind generally" (*DQC* 79); whereas wine "disorders the mental faculties," opium "introduces amongst them the most exquisite order, legislation and harmony" (*DQC* 73). The essential effect of opium is to restore the condition of the finely balanced nervous system to a condition of homeostasis: for this reason we need not read De Quincey's account of its "controlling power" over "nervous irritation" or its efficacy as an anodyne and "tranquillizer of nervous and anomalous sensations" as contradicting its primary function as a stimulant (*DQC* 212). This primary function resolves the condition described by Foucault in *Madness and Civilization* as "a sensibility which is not sensation," when "the sensibility of the nervous organ itself overcharged the soul's capacity to feel, and appropriated for its own advantage the multiplicity of sensations aroused by its extreme mobility ... Since madness [the extreme form of nervous maladjustment] can be dumb immobility, obstinate fixation as well as disorder and agitation, the cure consists in reviving in the sufferer a movement that will be both regular and real, in the sense that it will obey the rules of the world's movements."[11] It is important to stress that the reality and regularity of the world's movements to which the sufferer is restored are precisely *not* the flux of incoming impressions (which have stretched and irritated the sensibility), but rather the capacity of the soul to feel and to reflect. Opium offered an *induced*, artificial recovery of the sort of natural equanimity sought by Rousseau or Wordsworth beyond the morally-debilitating forms of modern sociability; as De Quincey put it, "a healthy restoration to that state which the mind *would* naturally recover upon the removal of any deep-seated irritation of pain that had disturbed and quarrelled with the impulses of a heart *originally* just and good" (*DQC* 74). As a form of inoculation (a word which De Quincey used in the *Confessions* to describe his own drug experiments) he recommends a controlled dose of stimulant to remedy a general over-stimulation, which has paradoxically resulted in what Wordsworth described oxymoronically as "savage torpor"; it is a homeopathic pattern recurrent in De Quincey's subsequent writings. Perhaps the clearest summary of De Quincey's representation of the Brunonian system was offered by the *Medical Intelligencer* in the review of the *Confessions* referred to above; it is moreover an account which we know De Quincey to have read as he cited it approvingly in the 1821 letter to the *London Magazine* (*DQC* 120):

> Opium is found, in the first place, to lessen the sensibility of the *nervous system*, and thus checks the transmission of sensations or impressions to the sensorium, whether painful or pleasant. The reduction of *sensation* in the brain and nervous system does not appear to reduce the activity of *reflection*; on the contrary, the intellectual operations are quickened under the influence of opium – a proof that its action is not uniformly sedative or stimulant on all parts of the system.[12]

The enduring importance of the Brunonian system in De Quincey's writing is nowhere more evident than in his numerous sketches of contemporary men of letters, as characteristic in the genre as Hazlitt's biographical sketches in *The Spirit of the Age*. Crabb Robinson's reaction to perhaps the most famous of these sketches, *The Last Days of Immanuel Kant*, identified this characteristic with great precision: "He has made much of the bodily constitution of a great man, with no allusion to his mind or philosophy."[13] Writing on Herder, "the German Coleridge," in the *London Magazine* for April 1823, De Quincey felt that "opium would have been of service to [the German writer]." He diagnosed his malaise as characteristic of his age, "weariness of daily life, inirritability of the nerves to the common stimulants which life supplies ... he was sick of the endless revolution upon his eyes of the same dull unimpassioned spectacle" (*DQW* 4: 384). The Herderian *Weltschmerz* is in stark contrast to the "exquisite" health of Immanuel Kant, as described in *The Last Days of Immanuel Kant* (in *Blackwood's Magazine* for February 1827). Until the philosopher's rapid mental and physical decline (marked by gnawing stomach pains for which De Quincey hypothetically prescribed "a quarter grain of opium, every eight hours" – *DQW* 4: 359), Kant's "great interest in Brunonian medicine" had ensured his enjoyment of a "state of positive pleasure-able sensation" and "the absence of pain, and of irritation, and also of malaise" (*DQW* 4: 339). Kant's famous solitary post-prandial walk was an important article of his adherence to a Brunonian regime, an example of the brisk exercise (as prescribed by Brown as an alternative or supplement to opium) which De Quincey elsewhere recommended as "omnipotent against all modes of debility or obscure nervous irritations" (*DQC* 208). Another figure who enjoyed a privileged, and like Kant, somewhat Oedipal, position in the De Quinceyan pantheon was Wordsworth, who thrived on the natural stimulus of walking rather than the preternatural one of opium, and was also a by-word for sobriety. In his 1839 article on Wordsworth in *Tait's Magazine*, De Quincey calculated that Wordsworth had walked a distance of 175–180,000 miles – rivalling even the eccentric Scots Jacobin and Pantheist "Walking" Stewart (the subject of another pair of articles), who had walked everwhere, including Tibet and back. Wordsworth's "mode of exertion," he wrote, stood him "in the stead of wine, spirits and all other stimulants whatsoever to the animal spirits; to which he has been indebted for a life of unclouded happiness, and we for much of what is excellent in his writings" (*DQR* 135). My present argument is an attempt to read the *Confessions* as an interpretation of the "bodily constitution" of Coleridge, or more exactly, of his *Biographia Literaria*, aware that its author, like De Quincey and unlike Wordsworth, was dependent upon the preternatural, rather than natural, stimulant of opium.

Not all of the *Confessions*' first readers were blind to an ulterior motive which supplemented its role as medical polemic; in one of his characteristic semi-insights Crabb Robinson found the work "a melancholy composition, a fragment of autobiography in emulation of Coleridge's diseased egotism."[14] Robinson refers to the *Biographia Literaria*, a work whose author sought, in the words of the book's epigraph, "to spare the young those circuitous paths, on which he himself had lost his way" (*BL* 1: 3). The *confessional* aim announced in this quotation from Goethe had remained unrealised, however, and Coleridge's book had encountered the world as, in his own words, an "exculpation" (*BL* 1: 5). On a formal, public level, Coleridge proclaimed his philosophical and moral system to be based on the Will, his aesthetics upon the Imagination, which he offered to theorize in the "transcendental deduction" of chapters 12 and 13, and his political system to be anchored on fixed principles, exposing the self-centred pragmatism of Jacobin and utilitarian "metapolitics." The actual effect of the *Biographia* on many of its readers was quite different, however, inasmuch as it failed to score a hit as public discourse; its defensive, querulous tone marked a personal style of the kind described by Robinson as "diseased egotism." Coleridge seemed to constantly undermine his stated aims before the reader's eyes: instead of a Will, he displayed his "constitutional indolence," "procrastination" and "mental cowardice" (*BL* 1: 45): instead of a transcendental deduction of Imagination he inserted a "letter from a friend" in the middle of chapter 13 which represented his theorisation as unintelligible and unpublishable: instead of demonstrating the steadfastness of his political principles and thereby "exculpating" himself from damaging charges of political apostacy, he indiscreetly falsified his early political and theological ideas in the light of his later position. Coleridge seemed to be laying himself open to charges of inconsistency such as those made against him by Hazlitt in his celebrated 1821 essay *On Consistency of Opinion*.

The worst attack on Coleridge came, ironically, from an erstwhile member of his own camp, the Tory John Wilson who, like his close friend De Quincey, had been a fringe member of the Lake School until financial misfortune had driven him to embark upon a journalistic career in Edinburgh. In a notorious anonymous review of the *Biographia* in *Blackwood's Magazine* of October 1817, Wilson tore Coleridge to pieces, at the worst employing scandalous charges of a private nature picked up when he had enjoyed the confidence of Coleridge and his friends. The review, which reiterated the charges of "inveterate and diseased egotism,"[15] surprisingly began in an elevated and lyrical vein before stooping to pick up the mud; it complained that the *Biographia* "does not contain an account of his Opinions and literary exploits alone but lays open, not infrequently, the character of the Man as well as the Author ... without benefitting the cause either of virtue, knowledge or religion [it] exhibit[s] many mournful sacrifices of personal dignity, after which it seems impossible that Mr Coleridge, can be greatly respected either by the Public or himself."[16] Coleridge would have been better off letting sleeping dogs lie; as an erstwhile member of the poet's (albeit outer) circle, Wilson knew the facts about Coleridge's political past as well as the squalid details of his drug addiction, to which the *Biographia* seemed, at least to the initiate, to make constant veiled references. Wilson placed the *Biographia* in the same class as Rousseau's *Confessions* and Hume's *Autobiography*: it "[tore] away the shroud which oblivion may have kindly flung over his vices and his follies ... instead of composing memoirs of himself, a man of genius would be far better employed in generalizing the observations and experiences of his life, and giving them to the world in the form of philosophical reflections, applicable ... to the universal mind of man."[17] Wilson was here probing a weak point in Coleridge's defences, for the *Biographia* did find itself obliged, on account of its own sense of having fallen short of its declared aspirations, to announce itself as a mere prolegomena to just such a work of public and universal relevance, namely a projected systematic work on the "PRODUCTIVE LOGOS" (*BL* 1: 136). Like the withheld "chapter on Imagination," the "critical essay on the uses of the Supernatural in Poetry" promised at the end of chapter 13 (*BL* 1: 306), and a host of similar schemes, the projected work lay beyond the capacity of the "damaged archangel," entangled in the tortuous contingencies and compulsions of a life of addiction, with its grim auxiliaries "procrastination" and "mental cowardice." When De Quincey announced a parallel work in the *Confessions*, the grandiosely titled *De Emendatione Humani Intellectus*, he was quick to confess that the work was a mere chimera; there was no attempt to "exculpate" himself from possible charges of irresolution because he was writing, after all, in the character of an "opium-eater," unlike Coleridge. De Quincey felt that the work was part and parcel of the visionary architecture of his opium dreams, and thus "it was likely to stand a memorial to my children of hopes defeated ... of foundations laid that were never to support a superstructure of the grief and ruin of the architect" (*DQC* 99).

Wilson's criticism of Coleridge is, I believe, an important link between the *Biographia* and the *Confessions*, and the close verbal parallels between Wilson's article and De Quincey's address to the reader at the beginning of the early version of the work are so close that it is remarkable that they have escaped notice. Indeed one is led to wonder whether De Quincey himself might not have been the author of at least the rhetorical *bravura* which opens the review, not at all unlikely given the pastiche composition methods of contemporary review articles and Wilson's frequent letters to De Quincey begging him for material either for *Blackwood*'s reviews or for Wilson's lectures after his rigged election to the Chair of Moral Philosophy at Edinburgh University in 1820.[18] The parallels between review and book endorse Crabb Robinson's interpretation of the *Confessions* mentioned above, enabling an identification of the *Biographia* as the occasion and pretext of De Quincey's work. One example will suffice: when De Quincey writes that "Guilt and misery shrink, by a natural instinct from public notice; they court privacy and solitude" (*DQC* 29), he echoes Wilson's point that "the true confessional is not the bar of the public ... there are feelings ... which, in the silence of solitude and of nature, are known only unto the Eternal."[19] What De Quincey sought to do was to *materialise* the *Biographia*, in his very title naming the term which Coleridge's need to "exculpate" himself had caused him to repress, and which his fellow opium addict believed to be the secret of the work's "diseased egotism." As Crabb Robinson realised when he read the 1856 *Confessions*, the earlier version of De Quincey's work was not really egotistical at all, mainly because it was *impersonal*: "not the opium-eater, but the opium, is the true hero of the tale" (*DQC* 114). Wilson complained that the *Biographia* "rambles from one subject to another, in the most wayward and capricious manner,"[20] a fact which made perfect sense to De Quincey, who read it as the narrative of an opium addict. In a term which De Quincey developed in his later writings, the *Confessions* was the "Dark Interpreter" of the *Biographia*, a "dark figure on [its] right hand, keeping pace with [it]self," *stimulating* its abstracted, self-absorbed precursor which seemed to be wasting itself in interminable reverie, and "revealing the worlds of pain and agony and woe possible to man."[21]

De Quincey's starting point was to address the issue of hedonism, a consistently negative term in Coleridgean ethics: "If opium-eating be a sensual pleasure, ... [I] am bound to confess that I have indulged it to an excess," exceeded only, he hinted, by Coleridge himself (*DQC* 30). De Quincey admits luxury to be the sovereign principle of his work, as it is the *secret* principle of the contemporary narcotic freemasonry, "the whole class of opium-eaters" including Wilberforce, Dr Milner, Lord Erskine, Henry Addington, Coleridge, Abernethy and Sir James Mackintosh: "I confess it, as a besetting infirmity of mine, that I am too much of an Eudaemonist: I hanker too much after a state of happiness, both for myself and others" (*DQC* 87). What distinguishes De Quincey from the others, he claims, is both a willingness to *confess* and furthermore to *advocate* in positive terms the pleasurable and therapeutic effects of the drug. Whatever the negative status of either eudaemonism or opium (as we shall see the moral and pharmaceutical terms are closely, and literally, linked) in the ethical or medical views of Wilberforce or Coleridge or Thomas Trotter, De Quincey, playing somewhat the role of the devil's advocate, admitted that "An inhuman moralist I can no more endure in my nervous system than opium that has not been boiled" (*DQC* 99).

When Coleridge first revealed the secret of his addiction to the young De Quincey in 1807 (*DQR* 43), it is quite likely that he mentioned the name of his Bristol mentor Dr Thomas Beddoes, partisan of Brunonian medicine and author of a "Life of John Brown" prefixed to the 1795 second edition of Brown's own translation of his *Elementa Medicinae*. Beddoes, like Erasmus Darwin, whose medical treatise *Zoonomia*, also based on Brown's system, exerted a strong influence on the young Wordsworth and Coleridge, recommended opium as both an anodyne and a stimulant; he is usually held responsible for Coleridge's own opium habit, although he had certainly experimented with the drug whilst a Cambridge undergraduate. The fact that the young Coleridge, like the mature De Quincey, had subscribed to the Brunonian system chapter and verse rather qualifies the terms of the acrimonious debate in later years as to whether the two men had first taken opium as an anodyne to relieve pain or as a source of pleasurable sensations. That debate, sparked off by De Quincey's accusations in *Tait's Magazine* after Coleridge's death in 1834, was based upon a false premise, although not one that would have been visible to the public in 1834. If both men had subscribed to the Brunonian theory of disease and cure, and shared Brown's underestimation of the addictive powers of opium, then there could be no moral reason for either *not* to have taken it. In Coleridge's case, however, experience of the "pains of opium" and, more importantly, a rejection of the philosophical materialism which underpinned Brown's system, had by 1807 caused him to reject it, although he would suffer in the most palpable terms for the rest of his life the effects of the "false theory" of his youth. This is clear from a notebook entry dated January 1830, quoted in Gillman's 1838 *Life* of Coleridge, a rejoinder to the *Tait's* article of 1834, which in turn drew from De Quincey the bitter attack in his 1845 article *Coleridge and Opium-Eating*. Coleridge blamed "the necessity of daily poisoning by narcotics" not on a quest for pleasure, but rather on "pain, delusion, error of the worst ignorance, medical sciolism." The latter clearly refers to the Brunonian system, closely linked as it was to radical materialism. He went on to imprecate "mercy on the author of the 'Confessions of an Opium Eater', if ... his book has been the occasion of seducing others into this withering vice through wantonness."[22] De Quincey is thus seen as an advocate of "medical sciolism" and therefore a voluptuary; by 1830 Coleridge could or would not distinguish between radical materialism and wanton self-indulgence. Already the *Biographia* had been unambiguous in its rejection of Brunonian medicine, however, praising the English physician Richard Saumarez's *New System of Physiology* (1798), whose "detection of the Braunonian system was no light or ordinary service at the time" (*BL* 1: 162–3). Like the attack on William Lawrence's definition of life as a function of organisation in Coleridge's *Theory of Life*, the voluntaristic scheme of the *Biographia* was dissatisfied with a system which "made life an effect instead of a cause," equating it, "the contradictory inert force," with the capacity for "excitability" or irritability, and the "exciting powers" as stimuli created by external forces.[23]

Because Coleridge wished to argue that Imagination (far from being merely a reflex of sense data, a product of *sensibility* as the condition of a highly refined nervous system) was "first put into action by the will and understanding, and retained under their irremissive, though gentle and unnoticed, controul" (*BL* 2: 12), he found it necessary to devote the whole of chapter 2 of the *Biographia* to denying "the supposed irritability of men of Genius." Coleridge's ideal of the unconditioned will, his quest for "exculpation," could never repress the dark truth which haunted it in the shape of the body, of physical dependency; De Quincey, a less convinced transcendentalist but fellow opium-eater could see that diseased, irritable body all too clearly between the lines of the text. De Quincey must have found chapter 2 redolent of the feigned innocence described by Foucault: "The innocence of the nervous sufferer, who no longer even feels the irritation of his nerves, is at bottom only the just punishment of a deeper guilt: the guilt which makes him prefer the world to nature."[24] Coleridge of course categorically denied the pathological account of genius; true men of genius are characterised by "sanity of mind" and "a calm and tranquil temper in all that related to themselves" (*BL* 1: 33). Whilst these men are clearly not irritable, there exists a class of "false" geniuses, the simulacra of the first, whose irritability is based upon "an ill conformation of body, obtuse pain, or constitutional defects of pleasureable sensation" (*BL* 1: 37). These are the modern hedonists, who seek in luxury a stimulus for torpid sensibility, who seek preternatural and worldly substitutes for their natural deficiencies. These men, of whom the opium-eaters clearly form a class, compose the great party of "mere men of letters," the "manufacturers of poems," and the anonymous critics "fit instruments of literary detraction, and moral slander" (*BL* 2: 42). Coleridge dissociates himself from this class, although he has not the confidence to place himself in the category of healthy, unconditioned, genius. He inhabits both worlds, and neither, being both a critic and victim of "false theory." As his pseudonymous "letter from a friend" in chapter 13 asserts, in a strikingly anti-Brunonian metaphor, "Arguments drawn from your own personal interests more often act on you as narcotics than as stimulants" (*BL* 1: 304). Coleridge first took opium as a *stimulant*, became addicted, suffered the "pains of opium" and rejected the "medical sciolism" and materialistic epistemology upon which the demand for stimulation was based. He found himself left dependent upon the narcotic effects of opium, manifest as a repressed guilt which constantly threatened the programmatic voluntarism of the *Biographia*. This he articulates with sufficent clarity for a fellow-addict like De Quincey to comprehend; he names his mysterious ailment as "constitutional indolence aggravated into languor by ill-health; ... procrastination ... mental cowardice ... which makes us anxious to think and converse on any thing rather than on what concerns ourselves" (*BL* 1: 45). Of course this admission ironically qualifies the content by the form of its argument; instead of talking about the exquisite health of men of genius, Coleridge talks only about himself and his own pathology, a clear instance of Robinson's "diseased egotism."

This is exactly what the *Confessions* sets out to show in denying every tenet of chapter 2's argument. As valetudinarian and addict Coleridge falls beneath every moral and critical standard which his work avows, showing himself the most "irritable" of authors (in the technical sense of one suffering from a morbid nervous system), but also his prognosis of the cause of his malaise is at best mistaken, at worst hypocritical. Coleridge followed the medical theory of William Cullen in identifying opium as a narcotic, rather than a stimulant, as the Brunonian, and De Quinceyan, argument would have it. This meant, paradoxically, that, while believing in free Will, he accepted the deterministic Cullenite opinion on the unbreakable nature of addiction. Coleridge had no warrant for trying to kick the habit. On the other hand, De Quincey, following the Brunonian line which stressed irritability rather than voluntarism, an essentially materialistic and necessitarian epistemology, insisted with Brown that opium was not necessarily addictive and thus *did* have a warrant to "untwist the accursed chain." Because this paradoxical relationship of the two addicts to their drug structures their relationship to each other, it is worth quoting in full a relevant passage from the 1856 *Confessions*:

> I, boasting not at all of my self-conquests, and owning no moral argument against the free use of opium, nevertheless on mere *prudential* motives break through the vassalage more than once, and by efforts which I have recorded as modes of transcendent suffering. Coleridge, professing to believe (without reason assigned) that opium-eating is criminal, and ... having, therefore, the strongest *moral* motives for abstaining from it − yet

> suffers himself to fall into a captivity to this same wicked opium, deadlier than was ever heard of ... A slave he was to this potent drug not less abject than Caliban to Prospero – his detested and yet despotic master. Like Caliban, he frets his very heart strings against the rivets of his chain. (*DQC* 144)

In the *Confessions* De Quincey *rewrites* the *Biographia* in a pathological rather than a normative moral/aesthetic register, showing Genius, Imagination, Will and Principle to be conditioned by the complex nervous organisation of civilisation and all its discontents. But also by its concomitant remedies, in particular the "preternatural stimulants" of opium on the body, or (as I discuss in a larger work, of which the present article is a part), luxury and its contemporary economic and political agent, imperialism, on the body politic. The De Quinceyan shift from exculpation to confession presupposes an abandonment of the particular claim to discursive authority which towers over the ruinous surface of the *Biographia*, the Will or "Productive Logos," exchanged now for an immanence in which the author addresses his public as, in Foucault's words, "the authority who requires the Confession, prescribes and appreciates it, and intervenes in order to judge, punish, forgive, console and reconcile."[25] Just as Hume and the Adam Smith of the *Theory of Moral Sentiments* had theorised civil society as a macrocosmic nervous system, a "structure of interacting sensibilities binding together and controlling the whole"[26] through sympathy, the De Quinceyan politics of authorship founded itself upon a legitimacy of *fact* opposed to a Coleridgean legitimacy of *principle*. De Quincey confessed to, and on behalf of, a public which sheltered in its hidden places a "whole class of opium-eaters," a freemasonry which bound with secret links the addicts of High Society to their numerous fellows amongst the working classes of the great industrial cities like London and Manchester (*DQC* 31).

Although the *Confessions* contains no mention of the *Biographia* its structural fabric and thematic development are, I believe, parasitic upon that book, from the sporadic biographical narrative of its early sections to the fragmented dream visions with which it concludes and which De Quincey described as the rationale of the whole (*DQC* 126). If De Quincey's parasitism bears out Crabb Robinson's judgement that "he is too much a disciple and admirer to have anything of his own" (although in the case of Coleridge the admiration was clearly inverted),[27] it surely qualifies the charges he levelled against the *Biographia* for containing "barefaced plagiarism" of Schelling in the 1834 *Tait's* article (*DQR* 40). De Quincey was attacking a plagiarist for plagiarism, knowing that he himself had plagiarised from his victim. But if De Quincey's attack on Coleridge is latent in the *Confessions*, he was literally spoiling for a fight in the *Letters to a Young Man whose Education has been Neglected* published in the *London Magazine* two years later. Challenging Coleridge to "sally out of his hiding place into a philosophic passion and to attack me with the same freedom," he considered that

> Such an exhibition would be amusing to the public. I conceive that two transcendentalists, who are also two [opium-eaters], can hardly ever before have stripped in any ring ... I wish he would leave transcendentalism to me and other young men; for, to say the truth, it does not prosper in his hands. I will take charge of his public principles in that point, and he will thus be more at leisure to give us another *Ancient Mariner*. (*DQW* 10: 21)

The many parallels between the *Biographia* and the *Confessions* are of course in part attributable to what John Beer has described as De Quincey's "slow reenactment of Coleridge's career,"[28] De Quincey's deliberate plagiarism of a writer he denounced as a plagiarist, although at the narrative level these parallels seem carefully crafted. For example, De Quincey's account of his schooling at the hands of his "Archididascus" Charles Lawson, headmaster of Manchester Grammar School, alludes to Coleridge's description of James Bowyer, headmaster of Christ's Hospital (*DQC* 36–7; *BL* 1: 8–11). Characteristic of the difference between the two texts is their representation of authority; Coleridge found a liberating common sense in Bowyer's authority (a kind of "anti-authoritarian authority"), whereas De Quincey was depressed by the "meagreness" of Lawson's understanding (*DQC* 33), and even more so by the master's neglect of his charges' health, an accusation considerably elaborated in the 1856 version. The abuse of De Quincey's delicate nervous system, and the neglect of his guardians (his father having died in 1793, when Thomas was eight), caused him to run away from school and wander "down and out" in Wales and London. This "fatal error of my life" (*DQC* 1856 163), which he in later years regarded as a sort of original sin, or fall from grace, resulted in permanent damage to his stomach from "sixteen weeks of gnawing hunger," a complaint for which he later (in 1813) began taking heavy doses of laudanum, thus ending the pleasurable "honeymoon" stage of experiencing the drug which he had first taken at Oxford in 1804 (*DQC* 35). Coleridge had also traced the aetiology of his current "mental disease" ("delving in the unwholesome quicksilver mines of metaphysic depths") to his comparable "friendless wanderings on our *leave-days* (for I was an orphan, and had scarcely any connections in London)" (*BL* 1: 16). If De Quincey mingled with "peripatetics," literally "street-walkers" or prostitutes like Ann of Oxford St, during his friendless wanderings in London (*DQC* 50), Coleridge preferred the company of peripatetics in the more accepted sense of "philosophers," so that he could "direct ... [the conversation] to my favourite subject, Providence, fore-knowledge, will, and fate." Indeed, Coleridge's comment on this "preposterous pursuit" (in chapter 11, he made his disapproval of philosophers on the streets quite plain) would seem more appropriate to De Quincey's starvation regime than Coleridge's philosophical discussions, which Coleridge described as "injurious both to my natural powers, and to the progress of my education" (*BL* 1: 16). Such characteristically overdetermined judgements on intellectual affairs are pathologised in De Quincey's account into gastric, nervous, and, possibly, venereal complaints.

A central issue in the literary representation of the self must be the philosophical question of personal identity. In a passage of the *Confessions* which indirectly reflects on the autobiographical manner of Coleridge and Wordsworth (whose manuscript draft of *The Prelude* he had been one of the few men of his generation fortunate enough to read), De Quincey described his visit to a Jewish moneylender named Dell in London – during his sixteen weeks of "gnawing hunger" – in quest of credit to support himself and repay his debt to Ann the prostitute who had sacrificed her last savings to preserve him from starvation. Because of his renegade status, he needed to prove that he was Thomas De Quincey, beneficiary of his deceased father's will; he also needed a possible escape clause, in case Dell attempted to alert his guardians to his whereabouts. Dell suspected him initially of counterfeiting his own identity in order to gain credit: "It was strange to find my own self, *materialiter* considered ... accused of counterfeiting my own self, *formaliter* considered" (*DQC* 55). The equivocation was temporarily resolved, and De Quincey's personal identity guaranteed, by his aristocratic connections Lord Altamont and his father the Marquis of Sligo. Dell promised him credit if he went to Eton to get a signed testimony from Altamont, whom the Jew hoped might prove a lucrative business connection. Arriving at Eton to find Altamont gone, the starving De Quincey managed to get a letter from his cousin Lord Desart: he returned to London but found that, not only did Dell refuse Desart's terms, leaving him penniless, but that he had lost Ann, whose patronymic he had forgotten to note. This episode, replete with anxiety concerning the instability of personal identity linked to a failure to repay a debt which may have caused the death of an innocent young woman, is vintage De Quincey. The loss of Ann in "the mighty labyrinths of London" is described as the "heaviest affliction" of his life (*DQC* 64); mapped on to the death of his sister Elizabeth and of the young Kate Wordsworth, it is fashioned and refashioned into the nightmare visions of his later opium dreams, described in the *Confessions* as well as *The English Mail Coach* and *Suspiria de Profundis*.

Reminiscent of De Quincey's problem of identity with the moneylender is Coleridge's account in chapter 4 of the *Biographia* of the logical solecism called a "bull." Discussing the problem of equivocation concerning the meaning of the personal pronouns "I" and "me," Coleridge warns of the danger of confusing the *Ego contemplans*, the *act* of self-consciousness constitutive of personal identity (corresponding to De Quincey's "self, *materialiter* considered") with the *Ego contemplatus*, "the visual image or object by which the mind represents to itself its past condition, or rather, its personal identity under the form in which it imagined itself previously to have existed" (De Quincey's "self, *formaliter* considered") (*BL* 1: 72). The importance of autobiography for both Wordsworth and Coleridge – particularly the latter – was in many places "exculpatory" insofar as it sought, by demonstrating a consistency of principle between present and past selves (very far from being a "given" in the contemporary ideological climate), to gain the *credit* of personal identity. Ideally considered, as exemplified by Wordsworth at full poetic strength, this entailed a nourishment of a tranquil and composed present self by the "vivifying virtue" of the past, like the *Prelude*'s "spots of time" where "feeling comes in aid /Of feeling ... if but once we have been strong."[29] Coleridge, less happy with objects or histories ("I may not hope from outward forms to win/ The passion and the life, whose fountains are within" – *PW* 1: 365), based his "Dynamic Philosophy" on the lynch-pin of the *Ego contemplans* or *act* of self-consciousness: "The self-conscious spirit ... is a will; and freedom must be assumed as a *ground* of philosophy, and can never be deduced from it" (*BL* 1: 280). In reviewing his past lives in the *Biographia* Coleridge sought to confound the associationist psychology of Hartley and others by theorising consciousness as an act of *will* rather than the aggregate of sense data and memory. In a related discussion, he subordinated the aesthetics of Fancy ("a mode of memory emancipated from time and space") to Imagination, a power "first put into action by the will and understanding, ... which reveals itself in the balance or reconciliation of opposite or discordant qualities" (*BL* 1: 305; 2: 16).

In the midst of his long critique of Associationism in chapters 5 to 8, Coleridge considered an episode which demonstrated the imperishable nature of "the reliques of sensation ... in the very same order in which they were originally impressed" upon the mind. Commenting on his chapter 6 anecdote of the polyglot German maid, he argued that past impressions could only be fully recovered in their original order by madness (the maid was afflicted by "nervous fever") or divine inspiration; the "*body celestial* instead of the *body terrestrial*" would "bring before every human soul the collective experience of its whole past existence. And this, this, perchance, is the dread book of judgement, in whose mysterious hieroglyphics every idle word is recorded!" (*BL* 1: 114). Whilst Coleridge factitiously relegated the return of the past to a form of preternatural consciousness, policed, as it were, by the free-will and "absolute self," De Quincey played upon the involuntary memory, an opium-induced "body celestial" (reminiscent of Baudelaire's "homme-dieu"), as the paramount law of mind. In the *Confessions* he alludes to Coleridge's passage in discussing "the dread book of account, which the Scripture speaks of, is, in fact, the mind itself of each individual ... there is no such thing as *forgetting* possible to the mind" (*DQC* 103). De Quincey would develop the *Confessions*' "dread book of account" in the "Palimpsest of the Mind" section of *Suspiria de Profundis*, where he is troubled by the "grotesque collisions of ... successive themes" threatening "the grandeur of human unity," as he is disturbed by "horrid alien natures" repeating, doubling and multiplying the self in *The English Mail Coach* (*DQW* 13: 347; 284). In the *Confessions*' "dark interpretation" of Coleridge's proclaimed "absolute self," the autobiographical will, the *Ego contemplans*, is rewritten as a structure of dependence which interprets the Coleridgean myth of origins as a recurrent narrative of suffering, loss, and addiction. De Quincey's past is unredeemable; the scene which returns to haunt him tells of a past in which the self is *already* revealed as a counterfeit, both of itself and of the sense impressions ineradicably inscribed upon it, "those profound revelations which had been ploughed so deeply into the heart from those *encaustic* records which in the mighty furnaces of London life had been burnt into the undying memory by the fierce action of misery" (*DQC* 13). Because the *Confessions* presents itself as a case-history rather than an "exculpation" it is dedicated to represent rather than efface the traces of the past, which in the *Biographia* are subject to the selective "task of retrospection and revaluation" of the Coleridgean imagination. De Quincey accordingly substitutes *irritability* for will as a narrative strategy: "Not in the energies of the will, but in the qualities of the nervous organization, lies the dread abstraction of – Fall or Stand" (*DQC* 129).

If opium stands in relation to De Quincey as a simulacrum, a substitute for personal identity, like the dark projection which hovers on the right of Symons the murderer as he rushes on his hellish career in *Suspiria de Profundis*,[30] the *Confessions* exposes what it represents as the fraud of the *Biographia*'s ontology by revealing Coleridge as De Quincey's opium-eating double.[31] Like Dell the money-lender De Quincey suspects his subject of "counterfeiting" his former self in order to gain credit; Coleridge has sought to transform the dark penumbra of addiction and his shadowy political past into a halo of imagination, representing his life as a consistent and organic unity by an act of interpretative will. There is not time here to examine the ways in which the philosophical question of personal identity becomes necessarily identified with the ideological issue of political apostasy, problematising Coleridge's claims to organic integrity. But from the viewpoint of the "Dark Interpreter," Coleridge's claims for political as well as personal credit, founded upon the postulate of free will, appear as the freedom to wilfully falsify the truth of the past self, the ineradicable ("encaustic") traces of which De Quincey reads clearly inscribed upon Coleridge's, as upon his own, bodily pathology.

In De Quincey's exemplary encounter with the money-lender Dell, proof of personal identity (the patronymic) is only supplementary to the aristocratic connections which underwrite his claims to credit. Coleridge's equivalent of De Quincey's surety Lord Altamont was Lord Liverpool, Tory Prime Minister, to whom in 1817 he sent a copy of the *Biographia* with a long and metaphysical covering letter. Although Coleridge's intervention was in some degree a response to the social and economic crisis of that year, he nevertheless based his statement of principles upon the authority symbolised by Liverpool and "the good sense of the English people, and of that loyalty which is limited to the very heart of the nation by the system of credit and the interdependence of property" (*BL* 1: 213). Although the system of credit backed by landed property might seem consistent with the Tory principles which De Quincey had propounded as editor of the *Westmoreland Gazette* in 1818–19 (and indeed with many of his subsequent political pronouncements), we should not be too hasty in taking De Quincey at his word when he described himself, in 1847, as "a specimen of the fossil Tory" (*DQW* 11: 403). The *Confessions* first appeared in the radical *London Magazine* in a deliberate snub to the Tory *Blackwood's* (with whose editor he had had a series of altercations), at a time when the memory of his dismissal from the *Westmoreland Gazette* by the paper's proprietors, acting upon the wishes of Wordsworth's patron the Tory MP Lord Lowther, was fresh in his mind.[32] In the money-lending incident, De Quincey actually *failed* to get credit on the strength of his aristocratic connections, despite the generosity of Lord Desart, Altamont's surrogate. The failure is metonymically linked to the loss of the nameless Ann, swamped by the myriad of faces composing the London crowd, and De Quincey's own fears of being submerged in an ocean of undifferentiated humanity. But De Quincey takes the opportunity of his failed credit to criticise the elevated station of society; he is proud to be the "son of a plain English merchant" and judges "a station which raises a man too eminently above the level of his fellow-creatures [as] ... not the most favourable to moral or intellectual qualities" (*DQC* 62). In one of his *Westmoreland Gazette* editorials, De Quincey was critical of conservatism of the Coleridgean type based upon *principle* which subordinated national feeling and opinion to a transcendental authority. "Principles in themselves are inert," he wrote, "but national feeling is the power by which only a people can be predisposed to bad principle, or by which good ones can be made operative."[33] As a "new" rather than "old" Tory, De Quincey viewed the body politic as an organism in the sense of a complex nervous system, governed by mutual sympathies rather than by a sovereign will. Drawing upon the eighteenth-century Scottish account of civil society as a nexus of commercial interests in which according to Smith "all things find their level," rather than the neo-Harringtonian civic humanist discourse which underpinned much of the political thought of Wordsworth and Coleridge, he regarded national "feelings and sentiments" as creating an autonomous system of credit (in the etymological sense of mutual confidence), at once "causative, diffusive, contagious and vital."[34] His discovery of Ricardo's *Principles of Political Economy and Taxation* in 1817 provided him with "an organic science (no part, that is to say, but what acts in the whole, as the whole reacts again on each part)" (*DQC* 99) which usurped the Kantian basis of his earlier thinking, a shift perhaps ironically articulated in the "Kantian" title of his projected work *A Prolegomena to all Future Systems of Political Economy*. De Quincey's discovery of the "dismal science" again challenged the position of Coleridge who declared that "Political economy ... can never be a pure science" (*TT* 198); he would later demolish the Coleridgean theory of taxation and declared that, like Southey and Wordsworth, Coleridge was "ignorant of every principle belonging to every question alike in political economy ... [and] obstinately bent on learning nothing" (*DQR* 42). De Quincey regarded capital as a stimulus to the body politic, like opium to the nervous system: his writings are full of panegyrics to its organic power, creating a network of communications across the nation forged by technological advance, first of the mail coach system, then by telegraphs and railways. *Travelling in England in the Old Days* (1834) and "The Glory of Motion" in *The English Mail Coach* (1849) hymn the pleasures (as well as the pains, developed in the "anarchies" of his dreams) of the age of capital. The former essay envisaged the expansion of the "system of intercourse" in terms which reveal its kinship to the organic science of Political Economy as celebrated in the *Confessions*; "then first will be seen a political system truly *organic* – ie., in which each acts upon all, and all react upon each" (*DQW* 1: 370).

I want, by way of conclusion, to look at one of the dreams which constitute the "grand finale" of the *Confessions*, and which seems to have particular relevance to the topic of the present article. De Quincey described the dreaming faculty as "the one great tube through which man communicates with the shadowy" and regarded its exercise as essential to counter-balance the social, technological and political revolutions of his age. "Left to itself," he added, "the natural tendency of so chaotic a tumult must be to evil; for some minds to lunacy, for others a reagency of fleshly torpor" (*DQW* 13: 335, 334). The dreams, assisted by the "preternatural" stimulant of opium, themselves represent the lunacy which they are meant to remedy, thereby operating in a *homeopathic* manner upon the mind; the "strength of lunacy may belong to human dreams, the fearful caprice of lunacy, and the malice of lunacy, whilst the victim of those dreams may be all the more certainly removed from lunacy" (*DQW* 13: 339).

I suggested earlier that the dreams represent a De Quinceyan inflection or (to use a more De Quinceyan term) involution, of Coleridgean imagination. If Coleridge's self-projection in the *Biographia* was controlled by an act of narrative will, De Quincey's dreams represent the author as *victim* and object of a remorseless involuntary memory, the "dread book of account" which proclaimed that "there is no such thing as *forgetting* possible to the mind" (*DQC* 346). Or rather, De Quincey's dreams articulate the hidden self-knowledge of the *Biographia*, manifest in the fragmentation which comes to a crisis in chapter 13. Coleridge's "correspondent" describes the "chapter on Imagination" as a "Gothic Cathedral in a gusty moonlight night of autumn," its argument like "the fragments of the winding steps of an old ruined tower" (*BL* 1: 301–2). De Quincey's dreams in the *Confessions* are also composed of fragments, because he has been unable to form the "whole burden of horrors which lies upon my brain" "into a regular narrative" (*DQC* 97). One of the most striking of these is based upon the celebrated etchings of gigantic classical dungeons by Piranesi entitled *Carceri d'invenzione*, which translates (uneasily) as "imaginary prisons." To be more accurate, the dream is based upon Coleridge's account of the etchings, because De Quincey claimed never to have seen them; he mistakes their title, calling them Piranesi's *Dreams*, and imagines them as "vast Gothic [rather than classical] halls." Groping his way up the massive Gothic staircase of the *carceri* De Quincey imagines he sees Piranesi himself: "follow the stairs a little further, and you perceive it come to a sudden abrupt termination, without any balustrade, and allowing no step onwards to him who has reached the extremity, except into the depths below" (*DQW* 106). The architecture of De Quincey's dream is an accurate represention of Coleridge's chapter 13 letter; his dream is the *Doppelgänger* of Coleridge's correspondent's dream (a correspondent who, it turns out, is none other than Coleridge shamming). The architect is Coleridge's double (Piranesi had executed the etchings "during the delirium of a fever"; was he also an opium-eater?), is De Quincey's double, is his own double, as the same figure is depicted on different levels of "the winding steps of the old ruined tower." The figure is always suspended at the moment before plunging into the abyss, and yet he is simultaneously figured plodding up the next stage. The dream is terrible not only because it figures a De Quinceyan "murder" of Coleridgean idealism. It is also terrible because it betokens the realisation that Coleridge is De Quincey's double, and that the symbolic murder of Coleridge is also a self-murder. The Piranesi dream clearly represents the Brunonian article of faith in detoxification (the *Confessions'* assertion that its author had nearly "unwound the accursed chain" of addiction) as an unqualified illusion. The drug which De Quincey still doggedly believed to be a stimulus turned out to be his permanent incarceration. When De Quincey died in 1859, he was still an addict; in a sense, Coleridge, who had himself died addicted 25 years earlier, had had the last word. The dream represents reality as De Quincey, like Coleridge, most feared it might in fact be, as the "lunacy" of pure repetition, dependence and contingency. The terror that haunts the Piranesi dream for De Quincey is that in murdering one's double, a "transcendentalist who is also an opium-eater," one might be murdering oneself. As he wrote in an article on Landor in 1847,

> Any of us would be jealous of his own duplicate; and if I had a *doppelganger* who went about personating me, copying me, philosopher as I am, I might (if the court of Chancery would not grant an injunction against him) be so far carried away as to attempt the crime of murder upon his carcase; and no great matter

as regards HIM. But it would be a sad thing for *me* to find myself hanged; and for what, I beseech you? For murdering a sham, that was either nobody at all, or oneself repeated once too often (*DQW* 11: 460–1).

NIGEL LEASK

NOTES

1. *Henry Crabb Robinson on Books and their Writers*, ed. Edith Morley, 2 vols. (London: J.M. Dent & Son, 1938), 2: 767.
2. Grevel Lindop, *The Opium Eater: A Life of Thomas De Quincey* (Oxford: O.U.P., 1985), 248.
3. Lindop, *Opium Eater*, 261.
4. *Thomas De Quincey: An English Opium Eater, 1785–1859*, Introduction and notes by Robert Woof (Cumbria: Trustees of Dove Cottage, 1985), 55.
5. Thomas Trotter, *An Essay, Medical, Philosophical, and Chemical on Drunkenness, and its effects on the Human Body* (London: Longman, Hurst, Rees & Orme, 1810), 46.
6. Trotter, *An Essay on Drunkenness*, 46.
7. Richard Caseby, *The Opium Eating Editor: De Quincey and the "Westmoreland Gazette"* (Cumbria: The Westmoreland Gazette, 1985), 130.
8. Trotter, *An Essay on Drunkenness*, 171.
9. Christopher Lawrence, "The Nervous System and Society in the Scottish Enlightenment," in *Natural Order: Historical Studies of Scientific Culture*, ed. Barry Barnes and Steven Shapin (Beverley Hills and London: Sage Publications, 1979), 25, 28.
10. John Brown, *Elements of Medicine*, 1795. Quoted by Woof, "Introduction," *Thomas De Quincey*, 54, 55.
11. Michel Foucault, *Madness and Civilization: A History of Insanity in the Age of Reason* (London: Tavistock Publications, 1967), 156, 173.
12. *Medical Intelligencer* 3, xxix (March, 1822), 117.
13. Crabb Robinson 2: 740.
14. Crabb Robinson 1: 267.
15. "Anonymous Review" (by John Wilson) of Coleridge's *Biographia Literaria*, in *Blackwood's Edinburgh Magazine*, 2, vii (October, 1817), 5.
16. "Anonymous Review," 5.
17. "Anonymous Review," 4.
18. Lindop, *Opium Eater*, 239. I owe this suggestion that De Quincey might have written at least the first part of Wilson's review of *Biographia Literaria* to Barry Symonds.
19. *Blackwood's* (October, 1817), 4.
20. *Blackwood's* (October, 1817), 5.
21. *The Posthumous Works of Thomas De Quincey*, ed. Alexander Japp (London: Heinemann, 1891), 1: 9, 12.
22. James Gillman, *The Life of S.T. Coleridge* (London: William Pickering, 1838), 250.
23. See *BL* 1: 163n for an account of Coleridge's interest in Brunonian medicine.
24. Foucault, *Madness and Civilization*, 157.
25. Michel Foucault, *The History of Sexuality: Volume One: An Introduction* (New York: Vintage Books, 1980), 62.
26. Lawrence, "The Nervous System and Society," 33.
27. Crabb Robinson 1: 137.
28. John Beer, "De Quincey and the Dark Sublime: The Wordsworth–Coleridge Ethos," in *Bicentenary Studies*, ed. Robert Snyder (Nomau and London: Uni-

versity of Oklahoma, P., 1985), 172.
29. William Wordsworth, *The Prelude* (1805), Book 11, lines 326–8.
30. *Posthumous Works of De Quincey*, 1: 9.
31. Quoted, Lindop, *Opium Eater*, 317.
32. Lindop, *Opium Eater*, 237.
33. Charles Pollitt, *De Quincey's Editorship of the "Westmoreland Gazette," With Selections ... from July 1818 to Nov. 1819* (Kendal: Atkinson and Pollitt, 1890), 38.
34. Pollitt, *De Quincey's Editorship*, 38.

To "Make a Bull": Autobiography, Idealism and Writing in Coleridge's "Biographia Literaria"

Coleridge's biographical and literary life was long in the making. Before 1815, the year of the book's composition, Coleridge's letters and notebooks abound with material which was eventually to be incorporated in the *Biographia*. As early as 1803, a notebook entry foreshadows what was to become the book:

> Seem to have made up my mind to write my metaphysical works, as *my Life*, & *in* my Life – intermixed with all the other events/ or history of the mind & fortunes of S.T. Coleridge. (*CN* 1: 1515)

Here, metaphysics is a writing "as": truth is to be written as "Life," while the writing of philosophy is to coincide with the writing of the self. In fact, the *Biographia* seems to be written to prove what for Coleridge is the cardinal point of philosophy: "The postulate of philosophy and at the same time the test of philosophic capacity, is no other than the heaven-descended KNOW THYSELF!" (*BL* 1: 252). In the *Biographia*, the deduction of metaphysical truth is co-extensive with the deduction of the self, and philosophy is written "as" autobiography.

But if Coleridge's text is autobiographical, the *Biographia* is at the same time *not* an autobiography. Speaking in the "Conclusion" of the story of his life yet to be written, Coleridge says: "for *write* it I assuredly shall, should life and leisure be granted me" (*BL* 2: 237). In Jerome Christensen's words, the *Biographia* is only "marginally related to the author's life and an authentic autobiography."[1] Literature more than life, the *Biographia* – and "S.T. Coleridge," its literary subject – will come to be *haunted* by the question of the "letter," as we will see. By focusing on Chapters 1–13 of the *Biographia* (the first volume of the book when it was published in 1817), this article will show how literary biography and metaphysics implicate each other in the text in such a way as to make the autobiographical "mind & fortunes of S.T. Coleridge" themselves the ground and prospective achievement of "metaphysical" subjectivity.

I

In Chapter 1, Coleridge writes that his name (partly arising from his association with Wordsworth and Southey) has been connected with ideas and opinions which he would not acknowledge as his own. To redress this, the *Biographia* is an "exculpation" (*BL* 1: 5) from false charges and dangerous misunderstandings, a reappropriation of his scattered literary being. "I have laid too many eggs in the hot sands of this wilderness the world, with ostrich carelessness and ostrich oblivion" (*BL* 1: 45–6), bemoans Coleridge, the literary and littered man.

A work of literary reappropriation, the *Biographia* also aims to introduce philosophical rigour into biographical miscellany, to convert scattered reflections into coherent principles. Though an account of S.T. Coleridge, the text is more importantly a statement of philosophical rules:

> It will be found, that the least of what I have written concerns myself personally. I have used the narration chiefly for the purpose of giving a continuity to the work, in part for the sake of the miscellaneous reflections suggested to me by particular events, but still more as introductory to the statement of my principles in Politics, Religion, and Philosophy, and the application of the rules, deduced from philosophical principles, to poetry and criticism. (*BL* 1: 5)

This deduction of "philosophical principles" and their application to poetry and criticism is designed to establish what Coleridge calls "fixed canons of criticism, previously established and deduced from the nature of man" (*BL* 1: 62). As he says of his drive to establish a coherent ground of metaphysical knowledge: "I laboured at a solid foundation, on which permanently to ground my opinions, in the component faculties of the human mind itself, and their comparative dignity and importance" (*BL* 1: 22).[2] For Coleridge, however, distinguishing the "component faculties" of the mind is of no value unless the *unity* which coheres the individual elements is also demonstrated: "In order to obtain adequate notions of any truth, we must intellectually separate its distinguishable parts; and this is the technical *process* of philosophy. But having so done, we must then restore them in our conceptions to the unity, in which they actually co-exist; and this is the *result* of philosophy" (*BL* 2: 11).

The "result" of philosophy is the demonstration of unity, and the name the *Biographia* gives to this unity is, famously, the "imagination": for poetry, according to Coleridge, is the *activity* of unity. "The poet," Coleridge writes, "described in *ideal* perfection, brings the whole soul of man into activity, with the subordination of its faculties to each other, according to their relative worth and dignity. He diffuses a tone, and spirit of unity, that blends, and (as it were) *fuses*, each into each, by that synthetic and magical power, to which we have exclusively appropriated the name of imagination" (*BL* 2: 15–16).

The *Biographia*'s philosophical desire, indeed, is the demonstration of this "unity" of the imagination, a unity which necessarily involves the unity of the imagining self. For if the *Biographia* seeks to gather together the dangerously scattered literary man called S.T. Coleridge, it also aims to gather together or bring into one a dangerously scattered *philosophical subject* – the philosophical subject who is dispersed wantonly in the materialist philosophies which Coleridge rejects. Of Hartleyan associationism, for example, Coleridge writes:

> in this alone consists the poor worthless I! The sum total of my moral and intellectual intercourse dissolved into its elements is reduced to *extension, motion, degrees of velocity*, and those diminished *copies* of configurative motion, which form what we call notions, and notions of notions. (*BL* 1: 119)

For Coleridge, associationist philosophy is the assault of chaos upon the unity of mind – and, as well as reducing individual subjectivity to the litter of matter, it also dissolves divine subjectivity into nothingness. Of another materialist (and, like Hartley, another theist) Coleridge asks: "How is it that Dr Priestley is not an atheist? – He asserts in three different Places, that God not only *does*, but *is*, every thing. – But if God *be* every Thing, every Thing is God –: which is all, the Atheists assert. – An eating, drinking, lustful *God* – with no *unity* of *Consciousness*" (Letter to Edwards; 20 March 1796: *CL* 1: 112–13). For Coleridge, "unity of Consciousness" raises God above the universe as a "heap of little things" (Letter to Thelwall; 13 October 1797: *CL* 1: 349), and similarly saves human subjectivity from its reduction to atomised, discordant "elements." In order to discover the principle of this unity, to discover beyond "the *Stuff out* of which we make our conceptions and perceptions" the "thinking faculty, by which we make them" (*CN* 3: 3708), Coleridge turned to the philosophy of Kant in the *Critique of Pure Reason*, where he sought an effective salvation for the "poor worthless I."

Kant's revolution in the first *Critique* was to posit the "transcendental" categories of space and time as forms of mental organisation which structure the very intelligibility of natural phenomena, even though objects as "things in themselves" – outside the "phenomena" which are intelligible to consciousness – remain beyond knowledge. Coleridge found an answer to his anxious question, "Whence comes, whence goes, the personality?" (*CN* 1: 458), in Kant's "transcendental unity of apperception"[3] – the process whereby disparate perceptual instances are brought together into unity by the mind, thus making it possible for the self to have a perception which it can call its own. In this light, it is not surprising that Coleridge says that Kant "took possession of me as with a giant's hand" (*BL* 1: 153), for Kant's critique offered a systematic justification of the "unity of Consciousness" which Coleridge so desired to establish. The self could be saved from being dispersed in a mass of "little things."

Coleridge, however, remained unsatisfied by what G.N.G. Orsini calls Kant's "basic dualism."[4] For, while Kant rigorously separated the *noumenon* (the "thing in itself") from the *phenomenon* (the thing apprehended by perception), Coleridge wished to bridge this Kantian gulf and embrace the *unity* of the mind and object in knowledge. Coleridge writes:

> In spite ... of [Kant's] own declarations, I could never believe, it was possible for him to have meant no more by his *Noumenon*, or THING IN ITSELF, than his mere words express; or that in his own conception he confined the whole *plastic* power to the forms of the intellect, leaving for the external cause, for the *materiale* of our sensations, a matter without form, which is doubtless inconceivable. (*BL* 1: 155)

As this suggests, Coleridge's epistemological eye was always turned towards the *object itself* rather than to its mere appearance or "form" in consciousness, and this drive towards the "THING IN ITSELF" is what animates his enthusiasm for Schelling in Chapter 12 of the *Biographia* – for Schelling goes beyond Kant's dualism in the name of a more thoroughgoing idealism.

Orsini says that Schelling argues "'the only example of absolute conformity of thought and object' is 'the I, or self-consciousness', where the object known, 'me', is the same as the subject knowing, 'I'."[5] But how does this relate to knowledge in general? Schelling's definition of knowledge (which Coleridge translates for him in Chapter 12) is that it is "the coincidence of an object with a subject" (*BL* 1: 252). In Schelling's thought, this coincidence amounts to the claim that "Nature" – in order for it, as an "object," to coincide with the mind as a "subject" in knowledge – is nothing other than *unawakened* mind, and that "mind" is Nature which has achieved consciousness of itself. Sara Coleridge translates Schelling's argument thus:

> the perfected theory of nature [is that] in virtue of which all nature should resolve itself into an intelligence. The dead and unconscious products of Nature are only abortive attempts of Nature to reflect herself; but the so named DEAD nature in general is an unripe intelligence ... even while yet unconscious, the intelligent character discovers itself.[6]

"Nature" reflecting itself, a latent self-consciousness in nature discovering itself: for Schelling, nature as mind/mind as nature enacts a process of becoming and self-creation in which "DEAD" matter is incorporated into living consciousness, and object is assimilated into subject. If Nature, in Schelling's philosophy, is assimilated to the horizon of consciousness, then the subject's or self's dispersal in the wastes of materialism is implicitly, even triumphantly, recuperated. Coleridge enthuses: "If therefore [the identity of subject and object in self-consciousness] be the one only immediate truth, in the certainty of which the reality of our collective knowledge is grounded, it must follow that the spirit in all the objects which it views, views only itself. If this could be proved, the immediate reality of all intuitive knowledge would be assured" (*BL* 1: 278). In his enthusiasm for

Schelling in the *Biographia*, Coleridge exults in the victory of self-conscious subjectivity: a victory, moreover, which offers both a secure epistemology and an ontology. And as we will now see, this triumph of the self effectively takes the form of subjectivity's autobiography.

II

During his critique of the atomisations of the self in Hartleyan associationism, Coleridge argues that without the self or will as a determining entity, certain dangerous consequences follow which threaten the intelligibility of the text he is writing: the intelligibility of the *Biographia* as an autobiographical text. He writes:

> According to [Hartley's] hypothesis the disquisition, to which I am at present soliciting the reader's attention, may be as truly said to be written by Saint Paul's church, as by *me*: for it is the mere motion of my muscles and nerves; and these again are set in motion from external causes equally passive, which external causes stand themselves in interdependent connection with every thing that exists or has existed. Thus the whole universe co-operates to produce the minutest stroke of every letter, save only that I myself, and I alone, have nothing to do with it ... (*BL* 1: 118–19)

Here, associationism abolishes the writing subject, together with the self who is the subject of autobiography. If the self, as Coleridge describes it in Hartley, dissolves into a "phantasmal chaos of association" (*BL* 1: 116), then the *Biographia* – on the Hartleyan system – would in a similar way dissolve into a phantasmal chaos of signification. As Coleridge describes it, the theory of the self is inseparable from the theory of the writing self: both are articulated at the same time. According to Coleridge, if I cannot be said to be *me*, I cannot be said to *write*. The same applies in reverse: if "I" cannot be said to write, then I cannot be called a self, and I certainly cannot be "S.T. Coleridge." In this way, Coleridge affirms the sovereignty of the philosophical self along with the sovereignty of the autobiographical self, S.T. Coleridge. These two desiderata, philosophy and autobiography, are virtually indistinguishable, for according to Coleridge philosophy *is* a kind of autobiography: "for herein consists the essence of a spirit, that it is *self-representative*" (*BL* 1: 278, my emphasis). Indeed, if this self-certainty cannot be assured, a dizzying void opens up in which "Saint Paul's church" might as well have written the text which I believe *myself* to have written – and any number of persons, things, impulses, nerves or motions could equally assert their claim. In this possibility, an absolute invasion of otherness usurps all claims of the self to sovereignty, and mocks the self with limitless irony instead of enthroning it in power. In Chapter 12, Coleridge asserts, "we ... can never pass beyond the principle of self-consciousness. Should we attempt it, we must be driven back from ground to ground, each of which would cease to be a Ground the moment we pressed on it. We must be whirl'd down the gulph of an infinite series" (*BL* 1: 285).

Along with his critique of materialism as the dissolution of self, Coleridge relates material *literality* to atomised subjectivity. For, considered in itself, writing appears to be a conspirator with materialism. A God overthrown by materialism, Coleridge asserts, is a God robbed of his meaning as absolute self and reduced to a set of phonetic and literal *marks*. The letter violates the spirit, as materiality colludes with literality:

> The existence of an infinite spirit, of an intelligent and holy will, must on [Hartley's] system be mere articulated motions of the air. For as the function of the human understanding is no other than merely (to appear to itself) to combine and to apply the phenomena of the association ... a God not visible, audible, or tangible can exist only in the sounds and letters that form his name and attributes. (*BL* 1: 120–1)

Here, materialism's assault on the paradigmatic self – divine subjectivity – is formulated as the self's abject reduction to the *merely* literal. Matter and letter come together to disperse divine subjectivity – and, by implication, human subjectivity, too.

However, this dangerous literality is always countered in Coleridge by a *good* literality which functions as the declaration, not the violation, of "spirit." The privileged metaphor for this declaration is nature's annunciation of the attributes of God, where nature as a sign or as a letter is assimilated to the powers of spirit:

> The theory of natural philosophy would ... be completed, when all nature was demonstrated to be identical in essence with that, which in its highest known power exists in man as intelligence and self-consciousness; when the heavens and the earth shall declare not only the power of their maker, but the glory and the presence of their God, even as he appeared to the great prophet during the vision of the mount in the skirts of his divinity. (*BL* 1: 256)

Here, the aim of "natural philosophy" is the demonstration of the *identity* of nature and divine intelligence. For Coleridge, the aim of "natural philosophy" is to demonstrate not just that nature *tells* of God (or is a sign of his power) but also that it *shows* God's "glory and [his] presence": it is a transfiguration which makes God "appear" as a presence (and not just as a Kantian *noumenon* or unknowable). In this sense, "telling" aspires to "showing," and nature as a sign or letter is appropriated to the *being and the presence* of the divine subject or signified. This play of nature as "sign" between a kind of telling and a kind of showing also appears in Coleridge's earlier poem *The Destiny of Nations:*

> For what is Freedom, but the unfettered use
> Of all the powers which God for use had given?
> But chiefly this, him First, him Last to view
> Through meaner powers and secondary things
> Effulgent, as through clouds that veil his blaze.
> For all that meets the bodily sense I deem
> Symbolical, one mighty alphabet
> For infant minds; and we in this low world
> Placed with our backs to bright Reality,
> That we may learn with young unwounded ken
> The substance from its shadow. Infinite Love,
> Whose latence is the plenitude of All,
> Thou with retracted beams, and self-eclipse
> Veiling, revealest thine eternal Sun.
>   (lines 13–26; *PW* 1: 132)

Half concealing, half revealing, nature's "alphabet" hovers here between telling and showing, representation and epiphany. Its alphabetic marks are themselves almost eclipsed in showing forth the brightness and *presence* of God. However, showing necessarily declines into telling as nature continues, platonically, to mark the *transcendence* as well as the evidence of God. On this scheme, however, nature's letters *do* declare the being of God and are superintended by his presence; they are a text which tells of his nature. Written by God, nature's letters discourse on their creator – functioning, in effect, as his autobiography. But Coleridge also envisages, in a remarkable poem entitled "Coeli Enarrant," the *failure* of this divine autobiography – where nature as a letter is "blank" rather than significant in its literality:

> The stars that wont to start, as on a chace,
> Mid twinkling insult on Heaven's darken'd face,
> Like a conven'd conspiracy of spies
> Wink at each other with confiding eyes!
> Turn from the portent – all is blank on high,
> No constellations alphabet the sky:
> The Heavens one large Black Letter only shew,
> And as a child beneath its master's blow
> Shrills out at once its task and its affright –
> The groaning world now learns to read aright,
> And with its Voice of Voices cries out, O!
>   (*PW* 1: 486)

This "O" announces both a cry and a nothingness, and abandons all symbolical readings of nature. The universal alphabet surrenders to a fearfully illegible mark – a "Black Letter." Like materiality before, literality functions here as an absolute *reduction* of being. If, in his moments of confidence, Coleridge sees nature's alphabetic *telling* forth (of God as meaning) as also a *showing* forth (of God as being), what the

Heavens "shew" here seems to be a literality from which meaning has been withdrawn, a materiality which can lay no claim to the privilege of being. Instead, the Heavens elude both significance and essence, and leave the self to gaze on them, as in "Dejection: an Ode," with "how blank an eye!" (line 30). In "Dejection," as in "Coeli Enarrant," Coleridge confronts the absence of what he calls "My shaping spirit of Imagination" (line 86): the spirit which moulds the matter of nature into significant form and reads nature's letters for their meaning – and whose truancy leaves him victim to a "grief without a pang, void, dark, and drear" (line 21). Indeed, the "shaping spirit of Imagination" is precisely that which the *Biographia* sets out to deduce and to demonstrate philosophically: a demonstration whose achievement involves both the affirmation of a *successful* divine autobiography and the self-positing of the *human* self – a self whose autobiography, in fact, the "Imagination" is.

III

In Chapter 11, Coleridge warns: "be not *merely* a man of letters!" (*BL* 1: 229). Jerome Christensen argues that this injunction should be "taken literally in the *Biographia* as Coleridge's statement of his most literal fear." Christensen writes: "Once he has been lost to print the man becomes a creature of the printing press, neither person nor thing, and subject to endless, mechanical reproduction."[7] Indeed, Christensen argues that Coleridge's self-exculpation in the *Biographia* from erroneous interpretations is a response to just such a fear: the fear of the self's dissemination in a waste of misunderstandings. As the authentic enunciation of the self, the *Biographia* seeks to redeem Coleridge from the dangerous *litter* of the letter. Literature or letters, in fact, is to be seen as a mere addition to the accomplishments of the self, and not its main prop: "Let literature be an honourable *augmentation* to your arms; but not constitute the coat, or fill the escutchion!" (*BL* 1: 229), Coleridge advises. That is, don't let literature constitute the ground of your being, the integrity of your selfhood, otherwise, the implication is, you will be mutilated in the ensuing battle, and the self will find no ground or place to constitute its sovereignty.

But how does this treacherous literality make itself felt in the *Biographia*? Might the *Biographia* itself conceal a "large Black Letter" which turns its readers away from it, frustrating their attempts at decipherment? How successful is the *Biographia*'s recuperation of the self littered in the wastes of materialism, of the self scattered with "ostrich carelessness" in the verbal sands of the world? These questions, unsurprisingly, come together in the famous deduction of the "Imagination" of Chapters 12 and 13; for each of these questions devolves on the power of the Imagination as a "shaping spirit," a spirit which shapes the world in the likeness of the self.

In Chapter 8, Coleridge writes that the mechanism of knowledge "assumes a power that can permeate and wholly possess the soul" (*BL* 1: 134), a power which organises the disparate or the distinct into the unitary. He argues that this unity of knowledge depends on the "coincidence of an object with a subject" (*BL* 1: 252), a coincidence which means that *knowing* must pass into, or be swallowed up in, *being* – and vice versa. In Chapter 7 he writes: "How the *esse* assumed as originally distinct from the *scire*, can ever unite itself with it; how *being* can transform itself into *knowing*, becomes conceivable on one only condition" (*BL* 1: 132–3). This condition, he says, is the fact that the "Sentient" – the "vis representativa" or power of cognitive appropriation – is "itself a species of being" (*BL* 1: 133). Knowing is a species of being, and Coleridge's idealism declares itself in the fact that the "self" is the principle of this consanguinity: "This principle [of identity] ... manifests itself in the SUM or I AM; which I shall hereafter indiscriminately express by the words spirit, self, and self-consciousness. In this, and in this alone, object and subject, being and knowing, are identical, each involving and supposing the other" (*BL* 1: 272–3).

If knowing and being are identical in the I AM, then so are telling and showing. In the I AM, discourse (the form of knowing) does not merely "tell" of being, but produces it. The I AM, in this sense, is the ultimate in performative utterances, for it includes or posits the being of which it speaks. In the I AM, utterance passes immediately into presence: knowing passes into being, discourse into reality. Coleridge argues that such absolute utterance finds its ideal expression in God:

> if we elevate our conception to the absolute self, the great eternal I AM, then the principle of being, and of knowledge, of idea, and of reality; the ground of existence, and the ground of the knowledge of existence, are absolutely identical, Sum quia sum; I am, because I affirm myself to be; I affirm myself to be, because I am. (*BL* 1: 275)

Coleridge's text, however, hesitates between attributing the identity of being and knowing to human subjectivity on the one hand, and divine subjectivity on the other. While, on the one hand, he says that he will express the "SUM or I AM" "indiscriminately" by the words "spirit, self and self-consciousness" – implying that the I AM is a human locution – he also, as in the above passage, reserves the significance of the I AM for God, splitting being off from knowing on the human level: "For to us the self-consciousness is not a kind of *being*, but a kind of *knowing*, and that too the highest and farthest that exists for *us*" (*BL* 1: 285). And: "We are not investigating an absolute principium essendi; for then, I admit, many valid objections might be started against our theory; but an absolute principium cognoscendi" (*BL* 1: 282). Not the least of such "valid objections," on this theory, might be the unavoidable conflation of God with man, should the identity of being and knowing in the I AM be seriously claimed for the human. Coleridge's idealism stops short of this point, retreating into orthodox theism. For indeed, God's privileged possession of the I AM, is nothing less than the proclamation of an absolutely potent discourse, a discourse which produces the being of that which it utters – where language creates reality, and utterance is one with presence. The I AM is God's supreme act of self-positing, declaring both his being and meaning in an absolute self-presence. God, in this sense, is the summit of the Imagination. The I AM is the perfect self-presentation of God's being in and as meaning and language: taken one way, it is the perfect autobiography, the language of the self become the life of the self, telling become showing.

Coleridge's laconic description of the Imagination from Chapter 13 situates the Imagination as a "repetition" of this perfect act of self-presentation or autobiography:

> The IMAGINATION then I consider either as primary, or secondary. The primary IMAGINATION I hold to be the living Power and the prime Agent of all human Perception, and as a repetition in the finite mind of the eternal act of creation of the infinite I AM. The secondary I consider as an echo of the former, co-existing with the conscious will, yet still as identical with the primary in the *kind* of its agency, and differing only in *degree*, and in the *mode* of its operation. It dissolves, diffuses, dissipates, in order to re-create; or where this process is rendered impossible, yet still at all events it struggles to idealize and to unify. It is essentially *vital*, even as all objects (*as* objects) are essentially fixed and dead. (*BL* 1: 304)

As a series of "echoes', the imagination is situated at a remove from God as Imagination's apex: the absolute "shaping spirit," the infinitely creative and self-creating I AM. As a secondary "repetition" of God, an imperfect imitation, the human imagination is marked by a *rift* between being and knowing which the divine performative, the I AM, surpasses. Coleridge's text constantly acknowledges this rift – even while its desire, fixed on the I AM, strains to abolish this split in the name of establishing the sovereignty or self-identity of imaginative subjectivity. He writes: "During the act of knowledge itself, the objective and subjective are so instantly united, that we cannot determine to which of the two priority belongs. There is no first, and no second; both are coinstantaneous and one. While I am attempting to explain this intimate coalition, I must suppose it dissolved" (*BL* 1: 255). Again: "the spirit (originally the identity of object and subject) must in some sense dissolve this identity, in order to be conscious of it: fit alter et idem" (*BL* 1: 279). In this way, knowing demands the *dissolution* of being in order to come into existence as knowledge – but at the same time it moves towards the reconstitution of being in the form of knowledge (or what Coleridge calls "spirit").

The necessity of this divorce between being and knowing, along with the implicit desire to overcome it, produces a series of powerfully equivocal accounts of how the "Imagination" works in the *Biographia*. For the imagination plays a double role in the text: as the privileged aspirant to the I AM, it contemplates the unity of being and knowing, but as a power of secondary order (a repetition, imitation, echo) it is open to error and misunderstanding. For example, the imagination – supposedly the epistemological ground *par excellence* as the "prime Agent of all human Perception" – is capable of leading the self *away* from being as well as towards it. Coleridge writes that "a cycle of equal truths without a common and central principle, which prescribes to each its proper sphere in the system of science" is "inconceivable," and adds:

> That the absurdity does not so immediately strike us, that it does not seem ... *unimaginable*, is owing to a surreptitious act of the imagination, which, instinctively and without our noticing the same, not only fills out the intervening spaces, and contemplates the *cycle* ... as a continuous *circle* ... giving to all collectively the unity of their common orbit; but likewise supplies by a sort of *subintelligitur* the one central power, which renders the movement harmonious and cyclical. (*BL* 1: 267)

Curiously, the series without a principle is repudiated not on the grounds of ontology but of epistemology, not on the grounds of being but of knowing. It is refused not because it is impossible, but because it is "inconceivable." The imagination "fills out the intervening spaces" – fills in the gaps – "surreptitiously": it plays a trick on perception and doesn't let it acknowledge that what is "conceivable" to the mind (as *knowing*) might be fundamentally discontinuous with what confronts the mind as *being*. The imagination, in this sense, becomes a duping and unreliable (if benevolent) consciousness, leading the mind into the possibly erroneous belief that the world is a reflection of its own epistemological categories. The imagination, that is, *behaves as if the unity between being and knowing was assured* – as if ontology were under the governance of epistemology – instead of acknowledging that there might be an unbridgeable *gap* between the two. But if the imagination is a gap filler, it is also the gap opener, for it "dissolves, diffuses, dissipates, in order to re-create"; it creates spurious harmonies, but also destroys these harmonies in order to create anew. The imagination, in this sense, seems to live *in the gap* between being and knowing; it fills in the gap but it also presupposes the gap, dissipating the presence of being at the same times as it strives to generate this being through its own activity.

Gayatri Spivak, writing on the play between knowing and being in Coleridge's text, says that the *Biographia*'s argument on the imagination moves to the point "whereby its presentation would (if it could) be identical with its proof."[8] That is, the argument proceeds to the point where its discourse (the "presentation") would be identical with the reality (the "proof"), where knowing would pass into being. As we have seen, Coleridge's text both desires and resists this final point – for presumably, insofar as the unity of knowing and being is enacted in the great I AM, for Coleridge to *conclude* his argument would require him both to say and to mean "I AM." In this sense, it is as necessary, as Spivak points out, for Coleridge *not* to finish his argument as it is necessary for him to maintain the identity of being and knowing as its ideal horizon. If the I AM is what is desired – as at once the perfect autobiography, the perfect "self-*representation* and self-*signification*,"[9] and the perfect philosophical articulation of the self – then the *Biographia* ingeniously denies the identity for which it longs.

Coleridge's text performs this denial by sending itself a letter, the famous letter of Chapter 13 from the "friend" who has read the chapter on the Imagination: in fact, Coleridge himself. The letter interrupts the text's flight towards the full deduction of the Imagination – with a series of complaints about the chapter's abstruseness, its unfamiliarity and its incongruity in a literary autobiography. Rhetorically, this Coleridgean self-interruption has a double function. On the one hand, it effectively straddles the gap between knowing and being – the gap, as we have seen, which the *Biographia* leaves unfilled but whose subsequent replenishment the letter promises. The "friend" writes: "Be assured ... that I look forward anxiously to your great book on the CONSTRUCTIVE PHILOSOPHY, which you have promised and announced" (*BL* 1: 302), a discourse in which the "speculations on the esemplastic power" will be in their "proper place" (303). As Spivak says, "it is [the] gap between knowing and being that the episode of the imaginary letter occludes,"[10] for the letter masks the *Biographia*'s falling short of its full desire. But the letter also *opens out* as much as stops up this "gap" – interrupting and severing the desired identity of the *esse* and the *scire*, being and knowing, as much as promising their union. In Spivak's epithet, the letter has a "cutting edge"; or rather, it cuts both ways. The letter maintains the full deduction of the Imagination as *desire*, while severing and truncating its realisation in the present. In fact, the letter seems to function uncannily *like* the Imagination; for, as in Coleridge's example of the unorganised series without a governing principle, in which the Imagination "fills out the intervening spaces," the letter both fills up a potentially abysmal gap and marks the place where this gap or danger opens out. In this latter sense, indeed, the Imagination rises up with a certain amount of sublime alarm: erupting – as in Wordsworth's crossing of the Alps (like a trope with the most ghostly of genealogies) – "from the mind's abyss."[11]

And in a sense, the Imagination *does* function alarmingly in the *Biographia*; for, in Chapter 13, it appears with monumental and legislative force in two dense and dizzying paragraphs whose power seem to be as much to tease the mind with speculations as to satisfy it with answers. Coleridge subtitles Chapter 12 "A chapter of requests and premonitions concerning the perusal or omission of the chapter that follows," and requests that the reader "will either pass over the following chapter altogether, or read the whole connectedly" (*BL* 1: 233–4). The reason he gives for this is that "The fairest part of the most beautiful body will appear deformed and monstrous, if dissevered from its place in the organic Whole ... even a *faithful* display of the main and supporting ideas, if yet they are separated from the forms by which they are at once clothed and modified, may perchance present a skeleton indeed; but a skeleton to alarm and deter" (*BL* 1: 234). In Chapter 13, Coleridge indeed presents us with a skeleton: the "main result" (*BL* 1: 304) of the celebrated deduction of the Imagination. Like a skeleton, Coleridge's summation of the missing chapter traces out the shape of a presence which is not there – and the chapter itself, stamped with its magisterial yet skeletal utterance on the Imagination, is itself strangely *there and not there* at the same time. However, if the chapter's "main result" does not "alarm and deter" it is, no doubt, because of the way the text maintains a complex play of desire and hesitation, presence and absence, around its crucial declaration; for if the imaginary letter marks the possibility of an abyss of severance between knowing and being, the text still supports the possibility that this abyss belongs to the *mind*.

The imaginary letter does, however, dramatise what Christensen called Coleridge's "most literal fear" – his fear *of the letter*. For if the friend's fictitious letter severs knowing from being, Coleridge's dread of the self's reduction to the merely literal is likewise a dread of *being's evacuation from language* – that is, of signification's being emptied of any claim upon existence. In such a situation, signs, letters and marks abound, but being for ever flees away. Language becomes, in Wordsworth's terms from the *Essays Upon Epitaphs*, a "counter-spirit," one of those "poisoned vestments, read of in the stories of superstitious times, which had power to consume and to alienate from his right mind the victim who put them on" (*WPrW* 2: 84–5). What Wordsworth calls language's "dominion over thoughts" (*WPrW* 2: 84), here, is dangerous because it oppresses the mind with unidealised exteriority instead of allowing the mind its transforming powers. Crucially, Coleridge's fictive "friend" himself is oppressed by such a victory of language over thoughts, by an alienation from his sovereign consciousness in a severance of language from reality in which signs become *unintelligible* to the mind. The friend complains that, reading the chapter on the Imagination, he was

> "Now in glimmer, and now in gloom"; often in palpable darkness not without a chilly sensation of terror; then suddenly emerging into broad yet visionary lights with coloured shadows, of fantastic shapes yet all decked with holy insignia and mystic symbols; and ever and anon coming out full upon pictures and stone-work images of great men, with whose *names* I was familiar, but which looked upon me with countenances and an expression, the most dissimilar to all I had been in the habit of connecting with those names. (*BL* 1: 301)

The friend's power to make interpretive connections fails, and unexpected relationships proliferate – all conspiring to bring about the defeat of his ability to make sense of it all. The friend remarks that "even if I had comprehended your premises sufficiently to have admitted them, and had seen the necessity of your conclusions, I should still have been in that state of mind, which in your note, p.72, 73, you have so ingeniously evolved, as the antithesis to that in which a man is, when he makes a *bull*. In your own words, I should have felt as if I had been standing on my head" (*BL* 1: 301). The note to which Coleridge's friend refers is from Chapter 4, where Coleridge describes the process of "making a bull" or a statement which involves unperceived contradictions. The example Coleridge chooses of a "bull," in fact, concerns the very discontinuity – between being and knowing – upon which Chapter 13 founders, along with the enthronement of the Imagination and the sovereignty of the self. Coleridge writes:

> There is a state of mind, which is the direct antithesis of that, which takes place when we *make a bull*. *The bull* namely consists in the bringing together of two incompatible thoughts, with the *sensation*, but without the *sense*, of their connection ... Thus in the well-known bull, "*I was a fine child, but they changed me*"; the first conception expressed in the word "*I*", is that of personal identity – *Ego contemplans*: the second expressed in the word "*me*", is the visual image or object by which the mind represents to itself its past condition, or rather, its personal identity under the form in which it imagined itself previously to have existed. – *Ego contemplatus*. Now the change of one visual image for another involves in itself no absurdity, and becomes absurd only by its immediate juxta-position with the first thought, which is rendered possible by the whole attention being successively absorbed in each singly, so as not to notice the interjacent notion, "changed", which by its incongruity with the first thought, "*I*", constitutes the bull ... Now suppose the direct contrary state, and you will have a distinct sense of the connection between two conceptions, without that *sensation* of such connection which is supplied by habit. The man *feels*, as if he were standing on his head, though he cannot but *see* that he is truly standing on his feet. (*BL* 1: 72–3)

In the "bull" which Coleridge describes the mind, like the imagination in the example of the series without a principle, erases the gap or difference between the two crucial elements in the sentence: the "I" and the "me." Eliminating the discontinuity introduced by the "interjacent notion, 'changed,'" the mind contemplates the "I" and the "me" as unitary – even though the word "changed" interposes a temporal disjunction which denies the "sense" of this unity. Just as the imagination worked "surreptitiously" to supply connections and create unities where there were none, so the mind here posits a unity by means of "habit." If Coleridge's "bull" welds the "Ego contemplans" together with the "Ego contemplatus" – the thinking I with the thought I, the *knowing* of the I with the *being* of the I – then one could say that the entire drift of the *Biographia*'s conceptual project is, in fact, to construct a kind of grand *philosophical* "bull." Moreover, as the principle which coheres the contradictory, the "Imagination" is the grandest "bull" of them all.

However, Coleridge's bull falls apart in the incommensurability between the "sensation" and the "sense" of connection (another version, indeed, of the difference between being and knowing). Because of "habit," the mind does not "notice" the problem inherent in the bull – it accepts a workaday conception of unity of being, and does not confront the epistemological and specifically *linguistic* ironies that afflict the statement. In the separation between the "sensation" and the "sense" of unity, knowing and being are again split apart, and the man loses all feeling of coherence – being left, it seems, only with the "sense" of a linguistic aporia. Like the friend who has read Coleridge's chapter on the Imagination, the man feels as if he were "standing on his head." Split between the "I" and the "me," the man's coherence of mind, unity of consciousness, and substantial being are fragmented into a grid of discrete and discontinuous linguistic instances.

Another example of Wordsworth's fear of language's "dominion over thoughts," this topsy-turvy moment in which the "bull" fails to work recalls the imaginary friend's oppression by the excess of language in Chapter 13, and his inability to *connect* the instances which confront him: "images of great men, with whose names I was familiar but which looked upon me with countenances and an expression, the most dissimilar to all I had been in the habit of connecting with those names." As in the unsuccessful bull, a reliance on "habit" and customary usage breaks down alarmingly. The habitual world explodes, and one is left standing on one's head.

Fittingly, then, the friend's resistance to Coleridge's discourse on idealist metaphysics takes the form of a plea for a *return* to the habitual, the customary and the quotidian. The friend writes that, should Coleridge publish the Chapter on the Imagination, his reader would "be almost entitled to accuse you of a sort of imposition on him" (*BL* 1: 303). "For who," he continues, "could from your title-page, viz. **My Literary Life and Opinions** ... have anticipated, or even conjectured, a long treatise on ideal Realism, which holds the same relation in abstruseness to Plotinus, as Plotinus does to Plato" (*BL* 1: 303). The friend petitions for a return to the habitual and customary self of autobiography, for the abandonment of the text's dizzying philosophical speculations on the nature of subjectivity. In this sense, the vertiginous intricacies of the knowing of the "I" are to be given over to the much more comforting assumption of the given being of the "I," in a safe return to the self of common autobiography. In effect, the fictive friend pleads for the *Biographia* as a text to "make a bull" *successfully* out of the human subject called S.T. Coleridge: to constitute him as a coherent autobiographical subject. What the *Biographia* reveals, however, is that – like Geraldine's singular and opaque "mark" in Coleridge's supernatural poem *Christabel*[12] – such an act of self-presentation is "A sight to dream of, not to tell!" (line 253; *PW* 1: 224).

STEVEN VINE

NOTES

1. Jerome Christensen, *Coleridge's Blessed Machine of Language* (Ithaca: Cornell U.P., 1981), 119.
2. Engell and Bate point to Coleridge's explicitly Kantian language here, citing a letter of 1811 in which Coleridge explains the similarity of his Shakespearian criticism to Schlegel's: "For Schlegel & myself had both studied ... the philosophy of Kant, the distinguishing feature of which [is] to treat every subject in reference to the operation of the mental Faculties, to which it specially appertains" (*BL* 1: 122).
3. For Kant's discussion of this concept, see *Critique of Pure Reason*, trans. Norman Kemp Smith (London: Macmillan, 1929), 135–61.
4. G.N.G. Orsini, *Coleridge and German Idealism* (Carbondale and Edwardville: Southern Illinois U.P., 1969), 189.
5. Orsini, *Coleridge and German Idealism*, 194–5.
6. Sara Coleridge's translation of this passage appears in *The Complete Works of Samuel Taylor Coleridge*, ed. W.G.T. Shedd, 7 vols. (New York: Harper, 1853–54), 3: 337.
7. Christensen, *Coleridge's Blessed Machine*, 31.
8. Gayatri Chakravorty Spivak, "The Letter as Cutting Edge," in *In Other Worlds: Essays in Cultural Politics* (London, Boston and Henley: Routledge & Kegan Paul, 1988), 9.
9. Spivak, "Letter as Cutting Edge," 9–11.
10. Spivak, "Letter as Cutting Edge," 9.
11. William Wordsworth, *The Prelude* (1850): Book 6: line 594.
12. For a remarkable reading of Geraldine's "mark" as a signature, see Richard A. Rand, "Geraldine," in *Untying the Text: A Post-Structuralist Reader*, ed. Robert Young (Boston, London and Henley: Routledge & Kegan Paul, 1981), 280–316.

Coleridge against Romantic Autobiography: Charles Lamb's "Letter of Elia to Robert Southey"

In number 21 of *The Friend*, originally published on 25 January 1810, Samuel Taylor Coleridge set down his views on biography as a prelude to a short account of his former patron and friend in Malta, Sir Alexander Ball, which was to appear in that and the following issues of the periodical. Coleridge's views were chiefly related to the by-then-traditional debate on the purpose of biography: usually it was maintained that it should serve some moral and instructive purpose and consequently a balance should be struck between the need to portray the public and the private individual, involving choices between revelations of behaviour which illustrated the subject's moral qualities and details which might offer psychological insights into his personality.

At the beginning of the nineteenth century, biographical theory and practice were still trying to come to terms with the new mode, finding heroic qualities in the life of the creative artist which needed to be documented towards completeness by the most detailed reproduction of the subject's actions and words, which had been largely inaugurated by Boswell in his *Life of Johnson* in 1791. Boswell's model demanded not only a mass of personal documentation but also the most complete recreation possible of the subject's social and intellectual milieu; the bringing back into focus of the artist and a whole dramatic totality of his friends. Many were alarmed at the prospect, and the sacred nature of private life was frequently invoked. Wordsworth and Coleridge were among the writers who were drawn into a rearguard action in defence of the individual's right to silence, but for a time the tide of public taste was running strongly against them, and the evident success of Boswell's great biography, both as a work of art and as a popular book, made his example hard to ignore. The upholders of reticence were in difficulties. But Coleridge did his best, as Wordsworth also does in his *Letter to a Friend of Burns*, to resist public pressure for ever-more-complete disclosures in biography:

> Lord Bacon ... evidently confines the Biographer to such facts as are either susceptible of some useful general inference, or tend to illustrate those qualities which distinguish the Subject of them from ordinary men ... An inquisitiveness into the minutest circumstances and casual sayings of eminent contemporaries, is

indeed quite natural; but so are all our follies ... The Spirit of genuine Biography is in nothing more conspicuous, than in the firmness with which it withstands the cravings of worthless curiosity, as distinguished from the thirst after useful knowledge ... how mean a thing a mere Fact is, except as seen in the light of some comprehensive Truth.[1]

Elsewhere, Coleridge, who clearly does not share Johnson's belief that there is no such thing as a fact which he would rather not know, speaks of "worthless anecdotes and petty personalities" and declares that "whatever facts and incidents I relate of a private nature, must for the most part concern Sir Alexander Ball exclusively and as an insulated individual." Like his subject when engaged in listening to improving conversation, Coleridge trusts that the reader will find his biography one of those which appeals to Reason, and that like the Bee, the reader will make honey while he murmurs.

However the readers of the day may have reacted, it is hard to imagine those of Coleridge's friends and contemporaries who ventured into brief biography or autobiography in the next few years murmuring with anything other than disagreement, for an examination of their writings only emphasises the extent to which Coleridge had been swimming against the current when speaking of biographical reticence and restraint. For most of Coleridge's fellows the exclusivity of the artist was of little interest: they simply did not see him that way. The artist immersed in the social and intellectual life of his time was what they sought to display, whether briefly or at length, and in doing this even apparently insignificant happenings or individuals might, if rightly understood, have their part to play in the process of psychological definition or self-revelation.

The years after Waterloo saw the writing, if not always the immediate publication, of several partial or complete autobiographies by writers. Coleridge's *Biographia Literaria* might operate chiefly in the area of intellectual self-definition, but the early drafts of Leigh Hunt's *Autobiography* or De Quincey's *Confessions* could scarcely be said to draw back from recording any but the most morally elevating incidents and relationships, any more than Scott's slightly earlier *Ashestiel Fragment* or (from what little is known of it) Byron's *Memoirs* could be said to do. But it is in the revived mode of the short biographical or autobiographical essay-sketch, now chiefly associated with the brilliant heyday of the *London Magazine*, that the most technically adventurous and psychologically original exercises in a biographical mode standing at the opposite pole from Coleridge's desideratum can be found.

From the earliest days of the *London Magazine*, in 1820, Charles Lamb contributed to its pages a succession of exercises in covert autobiography under the pseudonym of Elia. Lamb was 45 when he wrote "Recollections of the South Sea House," drawing on memories of his first months of employment in the City almost 30 years earlier.

From then onwards equally autobiographical, only lightly-fictionalised material, regularly formed the basis for his contributions as he recreated his schooldays, early holidays, the theatre at the turn of the century, or his earliest recollections of life at home and in the gardens of the Inner Temple. In 1823 the first of the two collections which make up *Elia* and the *Last Essays of Elia* appeared. At that time the flow of Lamb's Elian inspiration was still unbroken: that year two of the richest of the autobiographical essays written from behind the mask of Elia were published; "Old China" (March) and "The Old Margate Hoy" (July). But then in October there appeared an essay which shares the Elian attribution but is very different in tone and manner from the others; and after the "Letter of Elia to Robert Southey, Esquire" the Elian sequence was interrupted for almost a year and (despite individual successes) never regained anything like its old regular momentum.

During the months when Lamb was exploring his own past, affectionately but with a persistent cast of melancholy, in the Elia essays, his friend William Hazlitt was pouring out an unfailing stream of personal opinion, topical comment and direct autobiography in essay after essay. Though the friendship of the two writers was broken for a time by Hazlitt's chronic quarrelsomeness, each read the other's work with the keenest interest. And in the early 1820s Hazlitt published some of his key essays in self-definition by relating himself to his friends and intellectual mentors in both the past and the present.

Hazlitt's essays of this period frequently touch upon, or consider at length, the intellectual, conversational and literary capacities of his friends. Charles Lamb, with his highly-developed appreciation of the importance of friendship, was unlikely to overlook the fact. The personnel of his own Elian essays and Hazlitt's dramatis personae more than once overlap in any case, and the great transforming presence in their earlier years is a shared one, Coleridge, who is rarely long absent from what they write. Hazlitt might have lost faith in the older Coleridge, and Lamb might be living on the memory rather than the actuality of their friendship for most of the time, but both essayists felt a deep and lasting debt to Coleridge for his help in forming their mature mental character. So when Hazlitt transformed an earlier diatribe into an unforgettable celebration of Coleridge's youthful power in "My First Acquaintance with Poets" in the short-lived periodical *The Liberal* in 1822, Lamb was sure to take notice. He read *The Liberal* first of all because it was edited by his and Hazlitt's friend Leigh Hunt. For Hunt's sake he could overlook the fact that it was being financed by Lord Byron, whose personality and poetry Lamb usually disliked. In this instance he discovered *The Vision of Judgment*, and despite the fact that its most prominent target was another of his friends, Robert Southey, the Laureate, he was disarmed by the poem's radical energy, sheer brilliance, high spirits and wit. That Southey was its target was a fact likely to bring the poem back to his memory the following year when he felt himself to have been subjected to an unwarranted attack from the Laureate's pen in the *Quarterly Review*.

Lamb appreciated Hazlitt's essays and Hazlitt responded warmly to those of Lamb. But a particular section of "On Familiar Style," first published in *Table Talk* (1821), may have set Lamb thinking. Hazlitt has been praising Lamb's mastery of "old English Style" and his being "so thoroughly imbrued with the spirit of his authors, that the idea of imitation is almost done away." After other words of warm praise, Hazlitt proceeds:

> The old English authors, Burton, Fuller, Coryate, Sir Thomas Browne, are a kind of mediators between us and the more eccentric and whimsical modern, reconciling us to his peculiarities. I do not however know how far this is the case or not, till he condescend to write like one of us. I must confess that what I like best of his papers under the signature of "Elia" (still I do not presume, amidst such excellence, to decide what is most excellent) is the account of "Mrs Battle's Opinions on Whist", which is also the most free from obsolete allusions and turns of expression –
>
> A well of native English undefiled

Lamb's slightly fictionalised autobiographical sketches among the Elia essays are usually characterised by that lightly-maintained quaintness and archaism which critics have always recognised. An essay may begin in a plain enough mode, as does "The Old Margate Hoy," the essay which immediately preceded the "Letter of Elia to Robert Southey, Esquire" in the *London Magazine* ("We have been dull at Worthing one summer, duller at Brighton another, dullest at Eastbourne a third, and are at this moment doing dreary penance at – Hastings!"); but the style will soon rise to the first of a succession of crescendi of ornate, rhetorical language:

> Can I forget thee, thou old Margate Hoy, with thy weather-beaten, sun-burnt captain, and his rough accommodations – ill exchanged for the foppery and fresh-water niceness of the modern steam-packet? To the winds and waves thou committedst thy goodly freightage, and didst ask no aid of magic fumes, and spells, and boiling cauldrons. With the gales of heaven thou wentest swimmingly: or, when it was thy pleasure, stoodest still with sailor-like patience. Thy course was natural, not forced, as in a hot-bed; nor didst thou go poisoning the breath of ocean with sulphureous smoke – a great sea-chimaera, chimneying and furnacing the deep; or liker to that fire-god parching up Scamander.

Lamb's tone varies from essay to essay, depending on his subject, but an imaginative reworking of old tropes and allusions, with a frequent appeal to the elder authors whom he so loved, constantly features as he explores the rich layering of memory and the subconscious, the sudden discovering of associations, which the apparently ordinary can constantly reveal. His stance is that of a writer who has never lost his reverence for past experiences and what might roughly be described as a child-like capacity for wonder. It was a capacity which Lamb shared with his friend Leigh Hunt and which the essay "Witches and Other Night Fears" (in which Hunt's son Thornton appears) links to the profounder grasp of the subconscious and the transforming power of the imagination revealed by the early poetry of Coleridge. It was not, however, a capacity noticeably shared by Lamb's other friend, William Hazlitt.

Hazlitt, nevertheless, was actively engaged in his own process of self-definition by recreating and analysing the key features of his own past and establishing the nature and significance of its most important relationships during the months when Lamb was most occupied with Elia. Since Lamb and Hazlitt shared many friends, and since Lamb himself appears in a number of Hazlitt's essays of the early 1820s, he was bound to pay attention to Hazlitt's reminiscences, with their thumbnail sketches of his friends. The interest which "My First Acquaintance with Poets" would hold for Lamb has already been indicated. Another essay which he seems to have read and remembered with particular relish was the double one "On the Conversation of Authors" with its second part "The Same Subject Continued" which first appeared in the *London Magazine* for 20 September 1820 and was reprinted in the *New Monthly Magazine* two years later. The second part opens with a lively account of the former "Thursday evening parties" at Lamb's which lists, tersely and with a sharp eye for private eccentricities and personal character, the behaviour and conversational style of Lamb's guests. Hazlitt's style is direct, thrusting, pointed, with his typical manner of using the dash to link together a sequence of brief assertions not to create a passage which rises to a climax or piles material together till it achieves the weight and power of a cumulative mass, but rather to suggest a flow of impressions, vivid, exciting, life-enhancing. The real climax comes when the rush of impressions has been brought to a halt:

> Those days are over! An event, the name of which I wish never to mention, broke up our party, like a bomb-shell thrown into the room: and now we seldom meet –
>
> "Like angels' visits, short and far between".

When Charles Lamb's long-time friend and correspondent Robert Southey found occasion to criticise his religious soundness in a paragraph of a review charting "Theo-philanthropism in France and the Spread of Infidelity" in the *Quarterly Review* for January 1823, Lamb was clearly rattled.[2] Southey's criticism is directed at the account, in "Witches and Other Night Fears," of how Thornton Hunt, who had been brought up free from stories of goblins, apparitions or the terrors of Hell-fire, still suffered from nightmares: a proof, in Lamb's view, of the innate nature of our nocturnal terrors. Southey, however, drew from this the far-fetched moral that "modern philosophy" had done for the poor child, who would have been safe if "trained up in the way which he should go" and made into an orthodox Christian. *Elia* itself was priggishly characterised as "a book which wants only a sounder religious feeling, to be as delightful as it is original."

Lamb's correspondence from the summer of 1823 shows him lamenting the probable effect of Southey's paragraph on the sales of *Elia*, but this was clearly not what troubled him most. E. V. Lucas' excellent notes to the essay which resulted show that Lamb was in part directing his indignation at Gifford, the *Quarterly*'s editor during the more than a decade in which he had been repeatedly attacked in its pages.[3] But the personal affront which he believed he had received from an old friend, and the element of hypocrisy which he believed it contained, obviously hurt most of all. The whole strategy which he adopted in the "Letter of Elia to Robert Southey, Esquire" when it appeared in the *London Magazine* for October 1823 clearly shows it. Lamb was touchy on the subject of his unorthodox religious views and Southey's remarks startled him into an essay of self-exploration and self-definition essentially in the Hazlitt mode, in which the nature of his earlier friendships and what they show about himself is the prelude to a scornful and indignant revelation of the apostacy of some key figures from his own past. The form recalls Hazlitt's essays: the use of Southey as prime hypocrite also recalls Byron's poem which shared with Hazlitt the pages of Leigh Hunt's ill-fated journal *The Liberal* – for once again, as in *The Vision of Judgment*, Southey's self-righteousness is duly crucified.

The "Letter of Elia to Robert Southey, Esquire" is unlike the generality of Elian autobiographical pieces in that it is written wholly in earnest. It lacks playfulness, whimsy and the artful use of fancy to explore the layering of personality and mental associations. Its use of memory is direct: confirmatory at first and then, as the essay goes on, accusatory when Lamb moves back from the recent past to the period when he, Coleridge and Southey were most closely allied as fellow-thinkers and believers. Their shared views in the middle 1790s lie at the heart of the piece.

Lamb's essay opens startlingly, with a direct accusation, stated baldly, with none of the customary Elian obliqueness which a reader of the *London* would have come to expect:

> SIR, – You have done me an unfriendly office, without perhaps much considering what you were doing. You have given an ill name to my poor Lucubrations.

An account of the *Quarterly* article and Southey's criticisms then follows, with reminders that in an age of religious hypersensitivity unsupported remarks were quite enough to end the reputation of a book:

> Through you I am become an object of suspicion to preceptors of youth, and fathers of families. "*A book, which wants only a sounder religious feeling to be as delightful as it is original.*" With no further explanation, what must your readers conjecture, but that my little volume is some vehicle for heresy or infidelity?

The passage then continues its series of complaints, ending with a picture of childhood, not, as in the recent "Dream Children" as an exercise in escapism, but as a literal reminder of the distresses of the Hunt family, which Lamb implies should have inspired Southey's compassionate silence if nothing else:

> Was it worth your while to go so far out of your way to affront the feelings of an old friend, and commit yourself by an irrelevant quotation, for the pleasure of reflecting upon a poor child, an exile at Genoa?

Lamb goes on to recapitulate the subject of several of the essays in *Elia* which make some reference to Christian observances. He claims that his purpose in each of them was orthodox. But he moves on to consider the nature of belief itself and his style becomes figurative as he pictures the condition of believers and honest doubters. His conclusion, where he drops back into plain and forceful (because unexpected) language, must have startled Southey as much as the conventional believers of the day:

> The contemplation of a spiritual World, – which, without the addition of a misgiving conscience, is enough to shake some natures to their foundation – is smoothly got over by others, who shall float over the black billows, in their little boat of No-Distrust, as unconcernedly as over a summer sea. The difference is chiefly constitutional.

Lamb develops this point by imagining what forms Heaven takes in the minds of individual believers (for him, movingly, a reunion with "the old familiar faces," implied by the self-quotation, is the most desirable ideal of all). Once more the capacity to imagine, or to feel certain, pictured in figurative terms, is brought back to the plane of individual characteristics, defined in plain terms:

> That one man can presume so far, and that another would with shuddering disclaim such confidences, is, I believe, an effect of the nerves purely.

The essay now relaxes its seriousness for a while, teasing Southey with his readiness, as had been picked out by Byron in *The Vision of Judgment* (which Lamb refers to at this point), to use the practices of religions which he despises, and even the traditional picture of the

Devil himself, as material for his prose and poetry. For a moment Lamb even seems to be echoing Byron's style in his great satire on the Laureate:

> You have flattered him [the Devil] in prose: you have chanted him in goodly odes. You have been his Jester; Volunteer Laureat, and self-elected Court Poet to Beëlzebub.

Other pointed reminders of Southey's past willingness to use the superstitions of Catholicism as picturesque fodder for his poems are added. The style grows increasingly close-argued, short-breathed, piling up stabbing, openly-ridiculing phrases:

> You pick up pence by showing the hallowed bones, shrine, and crucifix; and you make money a second time by exposing the trick of them afterwards. You carry your verse to Castle Angelo for sale in the morning; and, swifter than a pedlar can transmute his pack, you are at Canterbury with your prose ware before night.

The style is effective: trenchant, vigorous and scathing. But it is not a style normally associated with Charles Lamb. It does, however, closely recall the chop-logic, stabbing mode, remorselessly picking holes in his opponents' arguments, which characterises Hazlitt's political reviews and sketches. And like Hazlitt, Lamb here affects a sometimes pitying but more often indignant scorn. He affects to enjoy Southey's jokes about other religions than his own, but it is the charge of bigotry which effectively sticks.

The link between Lamb's prose style and Hazlitt's becomes more manifest when Lamb takes exception to Southey's reported remark that he values him in spite of his friends, and goes on to list them, briefly pinpointing what it is about each of them that he values. The resemblance to Hazlitt's catalogue in "On the Conversation of Authors: the Same Subject Continued" is striking, though not perhaps altogether surprising, since Hazlitt was, after all, describing the Lamb circle as he remembered it from a few years earlier. Naturally there is a certain amount of overlapping: as in Hazlitt's list, not all of Lamb's valued friends (though some were undoubtedly great men) were prized for great deeds or remarkable opinions. William Ayrton, the music critic, characterised by Hazlitt as "the Will Honeycomb of our set" takes his place in Lamb's list as

> the last and steadiest left to me of that little knot of whist-players, that used to assemble weekly, for so many years, at the Queen's Gate (you remember them, Sir?) and called Admiral Burney friend.

The tone of Lamb's reminiscence is recognisably in tune with Hazlitt's

> When a stranger came in, it was not asked, "Has he written anything?" – we were above that pedantry; but we waited to see what he could do. If he could take a hand at piquet, he was

welcome to sit down. If a person liked anything, if he took snuff heartily, it was sufficient.

The two groups, one at Admiral Burney's, the other in Lamb's own rooms, stand at the opposite extreme from Coleridge's lofty conception of fit subjects for biography. Yet each essayist thinks them worth recording; has found them important for the definition of his own character as a person, a moral being and a writer; and each includes Coleridge among the dramatis personae of his group. Hazlitt's Coleridge is the older man, no longer the brilliant assimilative reshaper of new ideas of "My First Acquaintance with Poets," but a tetchier, more self-important figure, the first to find out new merit and proclaim it to the world, but the first, too, to disown it when popular acclaim follows. Lamb's is a more tolerant view, but one interestingly distanced in time; and interesting, too, in its implications within the context of his essay.

> An inquisitiveness into the minutest circumstances and casual sayings of eminent contemporaries, is indeed quite natural; but so are all our follies, and the more natural they are, the more caution should we exert in guarding against them. To scribble Trifles even on the perishable glass of an Inn window, is the mark of an Idler.

So Coleridge pontificated in *The Friend*. His appearance in the catalogue of Lamb's friends in the "Letter of Elia to Robert Southey, Esquire" might almost be taken (given Lamb's admiration for Coleridge's work) to show Lamb cocking an affectionate snook at his friend's portentousness, for it is through an inn window that Coleridge is seen:

> and Coleridge himself, the same to me still, as in those old evenings, when we used to sit and speculate (do you remember them, Sir?) at our old Salutation tavern, upon Pantisocracy and golden days to come on earth.

This is the first point in Lamb's essay where Southey is directly linked into his reminiscences: but from now on he is never allowed to forget that they have shared a past. A past, too, which was, in the Salutation and Cat days, dominated by Coleridge, who converted Southey (but not Lamb) to Pantisocracy, and also converted him (equally temporarily) to Unitarianism, a religious system which he already shared with Lamb. By 1823 it was a past which Coleridge flatly denied and Southey did his best to bury. Only Lamb had held firm, his views growing organically out of the beliefs of his youth. The reminiscence of "our old Salutation tavern" is not a coded one, since it is openly associated with Pantisocratic and millenarian enthusiasms, but it carries within itself the unspoken message that Lamb remembers plenty of other things that Southey might not wish to be reminded of, or Coleridge either, and that Lamb has no elevated views about biographical reticence to restrain him if further provoked.

The heart of Lamb's argument is now reached. He declared his belief that Southey would find little fault with the friends so far named, but refuses to abandon the two that Southey would most certainly take exception to, Leigh Hunt and Hazlitt. Lamb's affection for his friends is based on a tolerant and appreciative responsiveness to their good qualities and a willingness to overlook the rest. He now preaches a sermon on tolerance to Southey, the moral and religious bigot.

First of all, however, Lamb treats Southey to a warning shot across the bows in the form of a dazzling demonstration of the false logic of one of Southey's passages in the review which criticised *Elia*; revealing the unsatisfactoriness of Southey's supposed proof of Revelation through a direct parody of his style:

> The unwearied diligence, the profound sagacity, and the comprehensive erudition with which the New Testament has been scrutinised, and its authenticity ascertained, cannot be estimated too highly; and we will boldly assert, cannot possibly have been conceived by any person unacquainted with biblical studies. But here, as in the history of the Mosaic dispensation, if the books are authentic, the events which they relate must be true; if they were written by the evangelists, Christ is our Redeemer and our God: – there is no other possible conclusion. (Southey)[4]

> But your latter deduction, *viz.* that because 8 has written a book concerning 9, therefore 10 and 11 was certainly his meaning, is one of the most extraordinary conclusions *per saltum* that I have had the good fortune to meet with ... and for 11, that there is *no other possible conclusion* – to hazard this in the face of so many thousands of Arians and Socinians, &c., who have drawn so opposite a one, is such a piece of theological hardihood, as, I think, warrants me in concluding that, when you sit down to pen theology, you do not at all consider your opponents; but have in your eye, merely and exclusively, readers of the same way of thinking with yourself, and therefore have no occasion to trouble yourself, with the quality of the logic, to which you treat them. (Lamb)

The climax of irrefutable good sense to which Lamb's parody of Southey's style leads is, of course, all the more effective because Southey himself had held Socinian views while under Coleridge's influence, as Lamb well knew, and might tell the world some day. Under the plain surface of Lamb's "Letter" lie the ominous threats that a long memory allow him to suggest; his relative silence is itself a proof of his tolerance to a friend who he believed had shown none.

The chameleon-like element in the "Letter of Elia to Robert Southey, Esquire" is not yet exhausted: the thought of his friends still affects the character of Lamb's style in what ensues. Turning now to Leigh Hunt, Lamb affects a Hunt-like playfulness in claiming to find distinct character resemblances between Hunt and Southey. He then returns to the original sore point, Southey's attack on Thornton's education, as shown in "Witches and Other Night-Fears," and uses a Leigh Hunt-like appeal to sentiment to make Southey feel he has been unjust:

> I wish you would read Mr H's lines to that same T.H., "six years old, during a sickness":
>
>> Sleep breaks at last from out thee,
>> My little patient boy –
>
> (they are to be found on the 47th page of "Foliage") – and ask yourself how far they are out of the spirit of Christianity. I have a letter from Italy, received but the other day, into which L.H. has put so much heart, and so many friendly yearnings after old associates, and native country, as, I think, paper can well hold. It would do you no hurt to give that the perusal also.

The whole manner of proceeding through a rather loosely-focused emotional appeal (how *could* Southey read a private letter to someone else, after all?) which so strongly looks forward towards Dickens, is very recognisably Hunt's own.

The defence of Hazlitt now follows, a memorable character-sketch, warts and all, in a style rapid, short-phrased and punching, like Hazlitt's own; it is also a self-portrayal as Lamb charts the ups and downs of their relationship:

> I never in thought swerved from him, I never betrayed him, I never slackened in my admiration of him, I was the same to him (neither better nor worse) though he could not see it, as in the days when he thought fit to trust me.

The passage flings defiance at Southey, but is all the more remarkable in its evident deep feeling in that if seen it would clearly annoy Lamb's most valued friends, Wordsworth and Coleridge, both of whom had long since cast off Hazlitt as a scoundrel. Perhaps the compliment to his own manner of writing, as well as the moving testimony to a lost friendship, inspired Hazlitt's response. "I think I must be friends with Lamb again," wrote Hazlitt in "On the Pleasure of Hating," and the friendship was soon resumed, never to be broken.

Reconciliation and tolerance have been the keynotes of the "Letter of Elia to Robert Southey, Esquire." The final section (the only part which Lamb reprinted, slightly modified, in the *Last Essays of Elia*,[5] drives home Lamb's points with what is virtually a parable of exclusion from one of the holy places of his imagination. Reminding Southey (somewhat ominously) that "the last sect with which you can remember me to have made common confession, were the Unitarians," and naming a particular Unitarian chapel with the unspoken implication that Southey knows perfectly well where it is, Lamb tells of how, even before Southey advised him in the *Quarterly* to regularise his religious views, he went to an Easter service at Westminster Abbey:

> As such religion, as I have, has always acted on me more by way of sentiment than argumentative process, I was not unwilling, after sermon ended, by no unbecoming transition, to pass over to some serious feelings, impossible to be disconnected from the sight of those old tombs, &c. But, by whose order I know not, I was debarred that privilege even for so short a space as a few minutes; and turned, like a dog or some profane person, out into the common street; with feelings, which I could not help, but not very congenial to the day or the discourse. I do not know that I shall ever venture myself again into one of your Churches.

Lamb goes on to remind Southey that "you had your education at Westminster" and therefore must have shared his own experience of gathering "much of that devotional feeling ... on which your purest mind feeds still" amid "those dim aisles and cloisters." The remainder of the essay points out how depriving the general public, and in particular the poor, of potentially religious impressions through the imposition of an admission fee impoverishes the spirit of present and future generations, whose imaginations cannot be fed. Lamb's theme now grows quintessentially Romantic, in particular Wordsworthian, with its stress on the importance of early impressions and the awakening of the imaginative powers if "the holiness of the heart's affections" is to develop its full power. Religious feelings arise in the heart: no amount of pontificating and solemn scolding can make a man feel the imminence of God. Lamb's style is now wholly his own: plain, direct, without artifice. Yet even here it is nourished by literary associations, in particular the well-known *Spectator* essay in which Addison reflects upon the tombs in the Abbey. Characteristically, however, simple earnestness is not allowed the last word: a final neat joke, a private one in effect, reminding Southey once more that the writer knows a good deal which a High-Tory Laureate of orthodox religious principles might prefer to forget, closes the piece. The schoolboy Southey, a rebellious lad by implication, might just possibly have been responsible for the only act of vandalism in the Abbey that Lamb ever heard of. Does he know what happened to the nose of the statue of Major André?

Lamb's "Letter of Elia to Robert Southey, Esquire" is one of the most remarkable of all the Elia essays. Anger and pain drove Lamb into self-exploration, in particular concerning his religious beliefs and principles, an area where he usually preferred to explore only gingerly and through an oblique consideration of the past. The result was a spirited defence of intelligence, wit and reverence achieved through the free use of the imagination over the kind of narrow and mechanical dogmatism that Southey's article represents. But at the same time the "Letter" was part of the Elian sequence, written in Elia's name in response to a criticism of the religious principles shown in the first collection of Elia's essays in a book. The previous balance between Charles Lamb and Elia is disturbed by the serious nature (in Lamb's doubtless oversensitive view) of Southey's attack, but Elian artifice, though apparently abandoned, is, in fact, now present in a new style: instead of adopting the tone of voice of Elizabethan and Jacobean authors, Lamb here recreates the styles of his friends. Hazlitt, Hunt, Southey himself (for in spite of his anger Lamb does not wish to destroy the friendship, rather to make Southey realise how thoroughly he has tested it, and also to make him face up to his own unwarrantable arrogance and practice of double standards) are all recreated through Lamb's voice as he considers their importance in his own life. In the end, if a break is inevitable, he will side with Hazlitt and Hunt, practitioners (however imperfectly) of free investigation and assertors of the freedom of the imaginative powers.[6] For they, like Lamb himself, have remained true to the insights of their own early lives. On the other side stands Southey, and as Lamb's covert reminiscences of the mid-1790s show, behind him stands Coleridge, revered friends who have, nevertheless, played false with the faiths and the promise of their own past.

Lamb's mimetic voice in the "Letter of Elia to Robert Southey, Esquire" gives the appearance of doing what Hazlitt asked of him in "On Familiar Style": it abandons the imitation of the old prose writers and adopts the tone of modern writing and modern speech. But Hazlitt's words contained an ambiguity which he can scarcely have been aware of, but which Lamb, in his new Elian guise as direct self-apologist, seems to have picked up. Slightly puzzled by the nature of Lamb's archaic style and unsure how and where to place his emphases, Hazlitt says that we shall never know the answers "till he condescend to write like one of us." This, when he comes to define the importance of his friends, is what Lamb quite literally does, adopting (a nice compliment) Hazlitt's voice for the most heartfelt section of his essay, his cry of desolation at being deprived of Hazlitt's fellowship because of their quarrel. Though less well known than many of the self-fictionalising Elian essays, the "Letter to Robert Southey, Esquire" deserves to be recognised as one of the classics of Romantic autobiography. It justifies triumphantly that "mania for busying ourselves with the names of others" and "trading in the silliest anecdotes" which Coleridge had refused to countenance as among the materials for biography, and demonstrates how the personalities of a writer's friends, even down to their tone of voice and written style, become absorbed into his own consciousness, so that he best expresses himself when drawing, like the honey-making bee of Coleridge's discourse, their individual murmurings into the living presentation of his own self.

WILLIAM RUDDICK

NOTES

1. *Friend* 2: 285–7. The present and all further quotations from Coleridge's "A Prefatory Observation on Modern Biography" are taken from these pages.
2. *Quarterly Review* 56 (Jan. 1823), 493–536. The title used here, which was given to this essay by E.V. Lucas, gives a good indication of its contents, but appears to be his own adaptation of the title of the French volume reviewed by Southey (a work by M. Grégoire) together with a summary of the review's main thrust of argument. The passage dealing with *Elia* occurs on 524.
3. *LW* 1: 476–85. Lucas' notes are a mine of information.
4. *Quarterly Review* 56 (Jan. 1823), 531.
5. The Westminster Abbey material, with a new introductory paragraph, appears as "The Tombs in the Abbey."
6. The extent to which Lamb was committing himself to his London friends and accepting the risk of a total break with Southey, Coleridge and Wordsworth is briefly but convincingly indicated by Stanley Jones, *Hazlitt: A Life* (Oxford: Clarendon P., 1989), 348–9.

For Product Safety Concerns and Information please contact our EU
representative GPSR@taylorandfrancis.com
Taylor & Francis Verlag GmbH, Kaufingerstraße 24, 80331 München, Germany

www.ingramcontent.com/pod-product-compliance
Lightning Source LLC
Chambersburg PA
CBHW070302230426
43664CB00014B/2615